TEXAS
TORNADO

Brad and Michele Moore Roots Music Series

University of Texas Press, Austin

TEXAS TORNADO

The Times & Music of Doug Sahm

JAN REID

with Shawn Sahm

Requests for permission to reproduce
material from this work should be sent to:
    Permissions
    University of Texas Press
    P.O. Box 7819
    Austin, TX 78713-7819
    www.utexas.edu/utpress/about/bpermission.html

⊚ The paper used in this book meets the minimum requirements
of ANSI/NISO Z39.48-1992 (R1997) (Permanence of Paper).

Designed by Lindsay Starr

LIBRARY OF CONGRESS CATALOGING-IN-PUBLICATION DATA
Reid, Jan.
    Texas Tornado : the times and music of Doug Sahm / by Jan
Reid with Shawn Sahm. — 1st ed.
        p.   cm. — (Brad and Michele Moore roots music series)
    Includes index.
    ISBN 978-0-292-72244-6

    1. Sahm, Doug. 2. Rock musicians—Texas—Biography. 3.
Tejano musicians—Texas—Biography. I. Sahm, Shawn. II. Title.
    ML420.S133R45 2010
    781.64092—dc22
    [B]   2009022651

Frontispiece: Photograph courtesy of Shawn Sahm.

First paperback printing, 2012

CONTENTS

Prologue: A Real American Joe   1

1. A Cajun Two-Step Tex-Mex Polka   19
2. Song and Dance Men   31
3. Summers of Love   41
4. The Real Old Texas Me   55
5. Crossroads   69
6. Austin after Dark   83
7. The Coast-to-Coast All-Star Bands   91
8. Are We a Group?   105
9. Soap Creek   111
10. Groovers Paradise   123
11. Country Boogie   131
12. Sometimes I Cry   139
13. Wanderlust   147
14. Borderlands   159
   Epilogue: Guitar Slim   171

   Selected Discography   187
   Index   191
   Index of Song Titles   199

TEXAS
TORNADO

Prologue: A Real American Joe

Doug Sahm loved Texas but was never married to the place. For one thing he despised the heat. He took its Augusts and hundred-degree days personally. At varied times Doug arranged his life so he could chill out in New York, Chicago, California, Oregon, the Missouri Ozarks, Scandinavia, British Columbia. He disliked airplanes but loved the open road. Doug once explained the itchiness that often overtook him in Austin, his adopted hometown. "I can't stand to get bored here. When you get bored here, and nothing's happening, you can get pretty weirded out. But if you can keep some kind of edge going—that's why I leave all the time. You know, jump in the car, get in my Cadillac and drive to Seattle, drive to Minneapolis, see the Dead, go to spring training. It keeps you going."

The Dead of his reference were his old friends of the Grateful variety, and he was an ardent baseball fan. His favorite team was the Chicago Cubs, though he also was known to cheer for the New York Yankees, the Houston Astros, and Toronto Blue Jays. He used to drive band members to distraction by blowing off regular gigs and arranging his life so he could go to Florida or Arizona to watch spring training. One year a casting representative of George Lucas, the famous producer of *Star Wars*, called Doug and offered him a part in a

The Musical Mayor of Austin.
Photo courtesy of Shawn Sahm.

sequel to *American Graffiti*. Eventually it worked out, and he landed a nice role in the movie, but friends who witnessed the conversation were thunderstruck. At first Doug told the caller from Hollywood that he didn't think it was possible—the shooting schedule cut into too much of baseball season. During the spring training jaunts he drew on his stature as an entertainer to outwit gatekeepers and hang out with the big leaguers in the clubhouses and dugouts. He spouted major league stats until people rolled their eyes, and his kids would moan with boredom and embarrassment when he spotted a night game in some town, any town, and stopped to watch teams of strangers play a few innings. He was like an insect drawn to the lights.

Doug's trademark mode of transportation was a Cadillac or a Lincoln Continental. One of his Lincolns was a model that had been used in the TV series *Hawaii 5-0*. Before hitting the road, he would load a variety of instruments and small set of amps, the little gourmet coffeemaker he carried everywhere, and about a dozen suitcases. He'd tie up hotel elevators, trapping other guests in the cramped space, because suddenly he had to stop and count the bags carefully, making sure he had them all. In transit he was always writing, scribbling down a line of conversation or a highway sign that caught his fancy. He might linger in Lincoln, New Mexico, gathering material for a song about the murderous jailbreak of Billy the Kid, or stop and pay his respects in an old Spanish mission the highway offered up. He was known to drive from Texas to California to get a haircut or relieve a toothache. One long sojourn in western Canada resulted in a new band, a new audience, an acclaimed record, and a tour of Japan. He'd drive out to the West Coast to see his friend Bill Bentley, a onetime Austin protégé and publicist who became a top executive in the recording industry. Bentley made him the head of "artists and repertoire" of a new independent label called Tornado. Doug would swoop into Bentley's office in Burbank and blurt, "Write this down, Billy, it's important," and off he'd ramble about how to sign and promote some new artist or band he'd found.

But sooner or later, when Doug went off on his gypsy sojourns, he would call his elder son Shawn, a guitarist who grew up playing and writing songs with him, and announce, "Coming home, son. You know what to do."

Though it was a three-hour round-trip for Shawn, he would zip over from his home northwest of San Antonio to his dad's place in Austin and set the lights and air conditioner just the way Doug wanted them, because when Pop came home he wanted to park the car and dash inside, no hassle and, especially, no sweat.

All the early signposts pointed Doug toward a career in country music. The Sahm side of the family had emigrated from Germany to Central Texas in the early 1900s, landing at Galveston and establishing farms near the small towns of Selma, New Braunfels, and Cibolo. Doug's paternal grandparents, Alfred and Alga Sahm, owned and worked a prosperous cotton and grain farm in the Cibolo area; Alfred supplemented that income by playing in a polka band called the Sahm Boys. Doug's parents were named Vic and Viva Lee Sahm, and his older brother, born in 1933, was also named Vic. Doug's father had married into a working-class family called the Goodmans. His mother had ten siblings. The men on her side of the family carried lunch pails to work and often found their recreation in honky-tonks on Friday and Saturday nights.

Doug's parents had eighth-grade educations. Like many people uprooted from Central Texas farms in a time of drought and bank failures, his dad sought work in San Antonio during the Depression, laboring as a carpenter's helper, and then he made a somewhat better living on jobs at an army air corps base called Kelly Field. They lived in a succession of small apartments and had very little money. As times improved for them they saved enough to buy an acre on the eastern outskirts of San Antonio. With his elder son's help, Vic Sahm built a frame house of about four hundred square feet. It had a privy out back. They had butane for heat and, in time, electricity for light, but attempts to drill a water well failed; the younger Vic would fill up a milk can with water at a service station while his dad bought gas and kept the attendant talking and looking the other way. The second son, whom they named Douglas Wayne, was born in San Antonio on November 6, 1941. A month later, the younger Vic Sahm heard his mother sobbing one day and ran inside to see if his infant brother was hurt or sick. She had just heard the news about Pearl Harbor.

One of the boys' grandmothers loaned the family enough money to add on a little side structure so they would have a room of their own. In time San Antonio spread out to them, bringing its running water and sewage lines. What had been mostly countryside built up around them in scattered neighborhoods of poor black people. Viva took and passed the test for a beautician's license; she and a friend offered permanents to women acquaintances in a little shop

Doug strikes an ornery pose with his big brother Vic, before Vic left for the Marines and Doug became Little Doug the entertainer. Photo courtesy of Vic Sahm.

and brought in a little more income. Shaded in summer by a crepe myrtle tree blooming in pink, the little house in east San Antonio gradually looked more and more like a testament to the ordinary and triumphant American middle class.

Doug Sahm's dad was never a musician, but he came from a family of accomplished players, and both parents knew that not just any little boy could watch a grown man play a guitar, go home, and make the family instrument produce the same sound. Doug cut his teeth on western swing, the Texas- and Oklahoma-born hybrid of hillbilly string bands and big-band jazz—dance music exemplified by Bob Wills and his band's big hit "The San Antonio Rose," first recorded the year Doug was born. He had some fine teachers and mentors, for even a boy wonder could not just teach himself to play the triple-neck steel guitar; it was a complicated instrument, with three different tunings required. According to his older brother Vic, Doug was diagnosed with a childhood heart murmur that kept him from boyish pleasures like playing baseball. But when he was six, to his parents' enormous pride, he won a competition to appear on a local children's radio show and performed a hit by the Sons of the Pioneers, "Teardrops in My Heart." That same year, on one of the earliest live television shows in San Antonio, he played two steel solos between elders' renditions of "Liebestraum" and "Cincinnati Dancin' Pig." Doug's brother Vic was serious about playing football and drag-racing cars, not music. (He looked, dressed, and combed his hair like

Little Doug the drugstore cowboy.
Photo courtesy of Vic Sahm.

James Dean in *Rebel without a Cause*.) But Doug taught him to play enough rhythm guitar to accompany him so they could perform while passing the hat at weekend dances, and Vic appeared with his little brother on Shreveport's hot barn dance show, *Louisiana Hayride*. Years later Vic would chuckle about his biggest moment in show business: "This young guy on the show came over to say hello. I wished him luck and all. He told me his name was Faron Young." Doug was featured on Mutual Network broadcasts out of Texas's storied cowboy town, Bandera. He played with Hank Thompson and Webb Pierce. He was invited to join the lineup of the Grand Ole Opry, but his parents didn't want him boarding with strangers in Nashville. They wanted him to finish school and grow up in their home in east San Antonio.

Doug's dad regularly worked evenings part-time at a dance hall called The Barn, helping a brother who was one of the owners. Another owner was a local disk jockey and country music personality known as "Poke Salad" Charlie Walker. Hank Williams would play at The Barn on his swings through Texas. As an adult Doug would reminisce about seeing Hank Williams play gigs when he was a little kid. "He'd be up there, and I'd watch people watch the face of this guy, and I'd just go, look at this, man, they just stand there spellbound. And I'd be spellbound, too, as he was singing 'Lovesick Blues.' . . . He was the biggest thing in the world at that time. And, man, we talked one time when they had this birthday cake for him, and he saw me play and he said, 'Boy, you can really play that steel. Don't ever quit.'"

Doug had just turned eleven when a relative took a snapshot of him wearing a cowboy hat and sitting in the legend's lap at Austin's Skyline Country Club in December 1952. He didn't look comfortable. He said he mostly remembered how skinny and hard the man's leg was. It felt like he was perched on a fence rail. Two weeks later Williams dosed himself with morphine and vitamin B-12 and eased off on his last Cadillac ride.

In 1954 a booking agent named Charlie Fitch launched a remarkable enterprise called the Sarg Record Company. Discharged from the military in San Antonio after the Korean War, Fitch had built a record store and little recording studio in Luling, an oil and farm town in rolling country east of San Antonio. The label is mostly associated with the doo-wop period of postwar music, but one of Fitch's claims to fame was turning down Willie Nelson's earliest known recording, "When I've Sang My Last Hillbilly Song." (Willie had recorded the demo over a used tape of a country station in nearby Pleasanton, where he then worked as a disk jockey. As Willie's career took off, Fitch reconsidered the wisdom of that decision and released it on his label—one could hear background talk of pork bellies and other farm commodities on a morning price report.) In 1955, Fitch failed to sell Doug's first song to the Mercury Record Company, which was then one of the music industry heavyweights, and put out on his Sarg label "A Real American Joe" and "Rollin' Rollin'" by Little Doug & the Bandits. The jacket copy said the junior high student was then four-feet-seven and weighed eighty-one pounds. The publicity photo showed him grinning and holding a fiddle against his ribs, attired in a fringed Roy Rogers–style shirt, western bow tie, and a white cowboy hat pushed back on his head. His voice was the unchanged soprano of a boy. He was just a barefooted lad, he sang, goin' fishin' with his dad—"*a real American Joe.*"

Doug never lost his affection and feel for the country-western tradition he was born to. He once remarked that he made up his mind to spend his life playing music the night he watched Lefty Frizzell punch out a drunk and jeering cowboy and then leap back onstage and resume singing. A friend of Doug throughout his days was J. R. Chatwell, a renowned country fiddler who played with the Czech-German bandleader and singer Adolph Hofner, a man known in the Thirties and Forties as "the Bing Crosby of Texas." Doug not only learned music from his mentor and pal; he got practical instruction on how to live the bohemian life. Doug called him "Chat the Cat." But even as Doug played with the country bands and wore the costume of a drugstore cowboy, he spent many nights holed up in his room with a cheap record player and a neighborhood pal named Homer Callahan who brought over 45 rpms by artists with names like Lonesome Sundown and Howlin' Wolf.

Rhythm and blues and its thrilling offspring rock and roll blared from powerful AM stations flung across the continent from New Orleans to Chicago, from Gallatin, Tennessee, and Ciudad Acuña, Mexico. The same year that Charlie Fitch recorded "A Real American Joe" on the Sarg label, Doug was mesmerized by the music and televised performance antics of Little Richard, and he got to see a live concert by Elvis Presley in San Antonio. Doug's brother Vic gave up his dream of playing college football and joined the marines; when he came back to his hometown he worked for a while in a post office, watching a

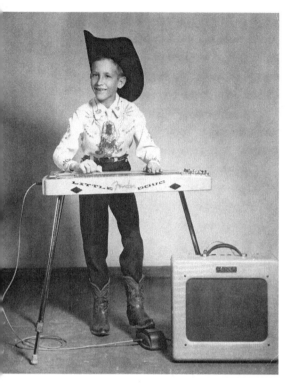

Little Doug the whiz player of the steel guitar. Photo courtesy of Shawn Sahm.

guy who for decades had been pitching mail in the same bin. Vic enrolled at Trinity, a local college, and studied business, which launched him down a completely different life's path—the brothers seldom saw each other and were not close. Doug's parents were relatively uneducated people who struggled to make a living; they were extremely proud to have a boy in the house who could attract such attention. The reflected limelight added to their sense of worth.

Doug began to sneak out of the house and prowl a few hundred yards to an exotic world inhabited by black people who danced till the sun came up. Across a ploughed field from their home was a dance hall called the Eastwood Country Club. "He took me there once, years later," said his friend Bill Bentley. "The show started at midnight, and the first band break was at four in the morning. What a night." The dancers writhed, whirled, and strutted to the rhythms and tempos of T-Bone Walker, Junior Parker, Bobby "Blue" Bland, Hank Ballard, James Brown. The white kid was so persistent, lurking out in the shadows, listening and trying to peek inside, that the owner, Johnny Phillips, let him come in and have a soda pop sitting off to the side of the stage. Doug's mother couldn't fathom what had gotten into the boy she called Bootie. The pedal steel prodigy who had smelled some of the last whiskey breath of Hank Williams was learning new dimensions of slide guitar from the great Chicago bluesman Elmore James.

Sarg Records promo for release of "A Real American Joe" by Little Doug and the Bandits. Photo courtesy of Shawn Sahm.

As Doug roamed farther about the city and deeper into its night life his parents occasionally threatened to pack him off to military school. He made friends with gifted young Chicano musicians on the city's sprawling West Side, and they introduced him to the traditions and music of the Texas-Mexico borderlands. They included Rocky Morales, who blew his tenor sax like he had the lung capacity of a whale, and Johnny Perez, a drummer and diminutive Golden Gloves fighter who decked troublesome guys on Doug's behalf on more than one occasion. The older "J.P." got, the cooler he got; he began to speak in rhymes. They joked with Doug that he was so Mexican he needed a proper name, and they gave him one, Doug Saldaña. Asked to perform at an assembly at Sam Houston High School in 1956, Doug was first warned by the principal not to do anything ugly. "They had this fear of rock, they didn't want anybody 'Blackboard Jungle-ized,'" Doug later described the gist of the principal's lecture. So of course he launched into a little Elvis routine, which got the curtain dropped right on top of him and all but set off a riot in the auditorium. In his senior class photo for the 1957–58 annual he wore a white sport coat, a dark, loudly striped shirt, a well-oiled pompadour, a grin full of characteristic bravado, and an oversized pair of sunshades. A cool cat and working pro.

One of Doug's high-school rivals became a lifelong friend. A year older than Doug, Augie Meyers was tall and dark-haired, and walked with a built-up shoe and a limp—one leg was shorter than the other. Childhood polio didn't allow him to walk at all until he was ten. Doctors wanted to amputate Augie's crippled leg, but one of his grandfathers had employed folk medicine, packing his limb with poultices made from the nests of mud dauber wasps. He had also been born with a malformed auricle of one of his ears. Music enabled him to overcome his self-conscious shyness.

Augie came from stock of rural Germans and Poles, whose tradition of the polka morphed into a distinctive norteño style of Mexican dance music that for centuries had been evolving in northern Mexico; the cross-fertilization of ethnic cultures stood out in communities of both sides of the Rio Grande, in the brush country called the chaparral, and San Antonio. Augie went to Brackenridge High School but dropped out. He said he realized that school and ordinary jobs were not his calling when he watched some Chicano boys playing rock and roll with the first electric guitars he'd seen. "My daddy spoke

Doug's photo in senior year for annual at Sam Houston High. Photo courtesy of Shawn Sahm.

great Spanish," Augie said, "and he loved Mexican music. He said, 'Boy, get you an accordion, and play that kind of music, and you'll go somewhere.' I'd say, 'Come on, Daddy. I wanta play like Little Richard or Jimmy Reed!'"

On East Houston Street Augie's mom owned a little store where the youth sacked groceries. One day in 1953 Doug wandered in and they started talking, not about music at first, but baseball. Soon Doug and Augie were breaking packages of bubble gum open to get cards of Doug's favorite major league stars. They talked periodically about getting together in a group, but they had their own things going. Augie eventually did learn to play the accordion, piano, and rhythm guitar very well, but he made his reputation playing the keyboards and singing backup for a popular teen dance band, Danny Ezba and the Goldens. Doug, meanwhile, was a hipster who fronted a succession of local combos called the Knights, the Mar-Kays, the Dell-Kings, the Pharaohs, and the Doug Sahm Big Band. "I came up in the sock-hop days," he reminisced. "Disk jockeys would let you play, and girls would go crazy. When you're fourteen or fifteen it doesn't matter that you're not getting paid." But he kept careful count of his progress. On sheets of notebook paper, he recorded in meticulous pencil each of his eighty-five gigs between October 1959 and May 1960—high school dances, NCO clubs on army posts and air force bases, the Green Hut in Corpus Christi, the Chicken Shack in Del Rio. The column on the right was headed "Bread." The most he got paid for any of those gigs was thirty-five dollars. Once he played two hours and made five bucks.

When he was twenty-two the massive audience swing to British rock and roll gave his vertebrae a profound yank and sent him in a new direction. Doug's breakthrough band was the Sir Douglas Quintet. All the members of the band were youths from San Antonio; Doug played guitar and sang lead and Augie poked the keys of a portable Vox organ. Briefly masquerading as an English group, the San Antonio band cracked the Top 20 of the United States and Britain with three hits between 1965 and 1968—"She's About a Mover," "The Rains Came," and "Mendocino." Those hits, which were recorded when Doug was in his mid-twenties, would be his biggest commercial successes, but his career bridged five decades. Among Texas musicians, only Buddy Holly, Roy Orbison, Janis Joplin, and Stevie Ray Vaughan rival Doug's importance in the evolution of rock and roll.

Just as he was gaining his initial fame, he ran afoul of the law in Texas and hostility directed at rebellious youths with long hair. On probation for what today would be a minor drug bust, he joined the mass youth exodus to California. "Them days," Doug said, "if you had long hair you could be risking your life. I remember one time we had to be escorted in and out of a town, touring with Little Richard and Jay and the Americans. I was saying, 'Please, sir, just let me go back to San Antonio, and I'll never come to Lynchburg, Virginia, again.'" He lived in California for five years and often claimed he didn't care if he ever set foot in Texas again. In November 1968 *Rolling Stone* ran an ensemble cover story about the Texas contingent in San Francisco music. The artist chosen for the cover was Doug; it could have been Janis Joplin. For the shoot, Doug wore his cowboy hat, a sport coat, and corduroy pants. Instinctively he grabbed his little boy Shawn, who wore hippie beads and his own cowboy hat, and set him in his lap, reproducing the image of that family snapshot of him perched on the leg of Hank Williams. Readers of the magazine knew nothing of that history, of course. But that was the year of the Bobby Kennedy and Martin Luther King assassinations, the Tet offensive in Vietnam, and American cities aflame in riots—and Richard Nixon had just been elected president. Was this longhair with the boy in his lap mocking people who revered country music and proclaimed themselves the Silent Majority? That's the kind of visual message that occurs to editors who design covers of magazines. But Doug was never much into politics. And he did have an undeniable claim to wearing a cowboy hat.

Staying true to his Texas roots and his early stage regalia, he invented or at least prefigured the fashion of the cosmic cowboys. Austin was still half a decade away from the cowboy hippie fad that blew smoke at the paranoia of the movie *Easy Rider* and the sneers of Merle Haggard's "Okie from Muskogee," and in the process established the Texas state capital as a major American music town. Playing a blend of country, rock, and blues spiced with the *conjunto* and *norteño* music of the Rio Grande borderlands, Doug articulated Texas country-rock, when he was in the mood for it, at a time when most of the hip world was enchanted with flower children, LSD, Haight-Ashbury, and the Summer of Love. And he was in the thick of all that.

When Doug came home to Texas in 1971, he and the mother of his daughter and two sons separated, tried to reconcile, and over several months came

1965 promotional photo of the original Sir Douglas Quintet. Manager and producer Huey Meaux evidently arranged for the shoot by Van Dyke Studios, in Beaumont, Texas. Photo courtesy of Shawn Sahm.

to the painful decision of divorce. For that and other reasons he chose Austin as a residence over his birthplace and fertile training ground, San Antonio. Doug's move to Austin set off a tremor that rivaled and coincided with the arrival of that charismatic Texas native son and Nashville dropout, Willie Nelson. Doug and Willie soon found a common groove in their music, their record label, and the weed they famously inhaled. But Willie's home was always his bus, as much as anyplace. Doug was a much more constant figure in Austin. Austin in the Seventies was a place where one could get stoned some afternoon, poke around the streets listening to music, and find inspiration in the form of a downtown junk store called Snooper's Paradise, which is how Doug conceived his song "Groovers Paradise." Doug called his band in those days the Tex-Mex Trip. He was literally all over the map.

Doug was widely loved, but he could also be a pain in the ass. He quivered and jabbered, all but threw sparks. The beatnik and hippie argot came spilling out of him in such a riffing torrent that some people recoiled from him, certain the fuel he ran on was mixed up in a bathtub in some foul-smelling house trailer. One of his Austin homes was in a tattered outlying subdivision notorious for its redneck hippies and speed labs. But he probably would have exploded if he had gone that route. He eagerly partook of the psychedelics he came across, and he sniffed up his share of cocaine when it became popular, but many people who knew him well—and were not always disposed to cast him in the best light—swore that his enthusiasm for those hard drugs rather quickly faded, and that his drug of choice was not amphetamines. Doug was regularly stoned on choice grass morning, noon, and night, but he blew right through the haze, running on heavily sugared coffee and a natural speed of metabolism, curiosity, and rebellion. It never occurred to him to change aspects of his lifestyle, once attained. One time his younger friend Joel Selvin, an author and rock critic for the *San Francisco Chronicle*, told him that he had gone straight and quit taking drugs. "Wow!" said Doug, utterly dumbfounded. "Why would you want to do something like that?"

For about five years in the 1970s, I chronicled the birth of Austin as a music center that was a junior cousin of Nashville, Memphis, and New Orleans. I controversially branded the style of play ascendant in those days "redneck rock," out of no more than a smart-aleck impulse and need of a book title. Doug brushed off a couple of my interview requests, and in *Rolling Stone* I would first read that he wanted to head up a tour of the cosmic cowboys, then very quickly he announced in the same magazine that people in Texas were tired of this shit and ready to rock and roll. I was one of those who thought he was indeed a speed freak, and how many of those do you really want to add to your conversations? I didn't know quite where he fit in Austin, and in the first edition of my book I didn't make as much of his importance and talent as I would when I had another chance. But I didn't write about any music again for two decades. So I never got to know him well, and I regret it. But my quitting the chase of backstage passes and loopy stoned interviews freed me to become once more a consumer of the wealth of music around me. That was when I gained a real appreciation of Doug Sahm.

Doug never quite got his due. He sold himself hard and was known to exaggerate. Part of him was a virtuoso and another part was a snake-oil salesman. There were times when his stock fell so low that he played in dives for crowds of fifty or sixty people. But he never lost his optimism or belief in his exceptional gifts. Doug played electric lead, electric bass, and triple-neck steel guitars; the fiddle; piano; organ; mandolin; dobro; tenor sax; and the *bajo sexto*, a Mexicano hybrid of bass and twelve-string guitars. The songs he chose to cover were as impressive as the ones he wrote. He was an ethnographer of old blues moans and country-western tearjerkers, and he was an aficionado of jazz. He had a wonderful sense of humor that always dwelled near the core of his music. Doug managed to construct his entire working life around playing music, and he lived well, enjoyed some wealth. He never had to hold a day job. How many musicians can claim that?

One of his brainstorms later in his career was the Texas Tornados, in which he led his old pal Augie Meyers, the crossover country and soul singer Freddy Fender, and the San Antonio–born accordion wizard Flaco Jimenez in a quartet that Doug pitched as a Tex-Mex reincarnation of the Beatles. The Tornados had a splendid commercial run and won a 1991 Grammy for a *conjunto* song in Spanish. But as a showman Doug was much closer to the Rolling Stones than the Beatles—a Jagger who could play, a Richards who could sing. Doug was a blur of continuous motion, and in moving so fast through life, in such a public venue, he achieved a measure of privacy. He thrived on being a moving target. This book is not offered as an all-embracing account that leaves no stones about his life unturned. I did not follow him all the places he went, did not track down all the friends he made, and a critique of his total creative output is not a realistic undertaking. Not counting the recordings on small labels that first caught radio listeners' attention in San Antonio, Doug is credited with more than 140 records released in the United States, Europe, and Canada; he played on or his songs were performed on albums by Willie Nelson, the Grateful Dead, Ringo Starr, Rick Danko, Augie Meyers, Steve Earle, Townes Van Zandt, Uncle Tupelo, Los Super Seven, and the Gourds, among others, and he contributed to the scores of several movies. My hope is to convey some sense of the antic swath that for decades he cut through many communities in many countries, to call up some voices of people who got to know him well, or at least chased after him and left the tape recorder rolling, and to demonstrate the sheer knowing of his music.

One afternoon in the late Seventies I watched him play a solo set beside a swimming pool for some friends of mine whose Austin restaurant had run out of luck and money. Without the accompaniment of the terrific bands he always had around him, I heard for the first time how fluent, melodic, and crystal-clear his guitar playing was. As Chuck Berry phrased it in that anthem of my generation, "Johnny B. Goode," he hit those notes and chords like he was ringing a bell. But Doug's musicianship was the lesser part of what moved me that day. He couldn't have gotten paid much for playing that gig. He didn't have to do that. It was an act of generosity and brotherhood, of bringing some happiness to what was otherwise a melancholy occasion. I thought: there's a man with a good heart.

Over the years, Austin changed in ways that annoyed Doug. He was so out of sync with the times in the Nineties that he still put people down by calling them squares. By the time he started obsessing about yuppies, even that expression was passé. For all the degrees from Stanford and M.I.T. and the gated mansions junking up the beauty of Austin's limestone ridges and gleaming lakes, most of those people were, in Doug's opinion, a bunch of high-tech dipshits. He had more in common with the cedar choppers that the developers rousted out of those hills.

Doug was a celebrated technophobe. For the first several years of his residence in Austin, he refused to have a telephone, on the theory that it wasn't

good to be too easy to find. He received his calls at a venerable head shop
called Oat Willie's, returning the important ones and billing the long distance
to patient friends who had the phone line there. Doug paced frenetically when
he was on the line. When he consented to have a phone installed in his name,
he was always getting a foot or a lamp stand or one of his cats tangled up in
his cord as he walked about talking. His children thought a cordless phone was
a great invention for him and bought him one as a gift one year. Doug didn't
trust it, didn't like it, couldn't figure out how to make it work, and in short
order he crammed it back in the box and told them no thanks.

One of Doug's few concessions to changing times and modern technology
was an answering machine with a message of famed elusiveness. It was blunt
and good-humored but very clear about the things that had the most meaning in his life. The message began with a clearing of his throat, then: "I'm not
home right now, I'm out milking the cows—uh, so, uh, [you] might call back if
it's, uh, baseball or Guitar Slim or something that's interesting. I'll give you a
buzz; have a good day. Adios."

A Cajun Two-Step Tex-Mex Polka

As he outgrew being *Little Doug,* he gradually stopped playing with his elders in country bands. He entered a phase playing with youthful rockabilly bands with names like Eddy Dugosh and the Ah-Ha Playboys and Rudy Grayzell and the Kool Kats. Grayzell had performed with Doug on the *Louisiana Hayride,* and he was old enough to drive. "I used to take Doug on tour in Houston and he tore the house down," he told one interviewer, Andrew Brown. "I used to pull up to Doug's school and tell 'em, 'I'm Doug's guardian and he's gotta come home right now.' They'd pull Doug out of class and I'd have my car out front with our guitars in the trunk. And I'd say, 'C'mon, Doug, I got us a show!'"

Doug hadn't entirely cut his ties with customary recreations of boys his age. He prided himself on his left-handed swing on the baseball field, and he joined his junior high marching band. But on nights when he wasn't going across the fields to the Eastwood Country Club, he started catching a ride to a smoky little bar in downtown San Antonio called the Tiffany Lounge. He hung out with a local blues singer called Little Sammy Jay, and soon he was playing electric guitar in Jay's shows, which led to a job with the band of the gospel and blues icon Jimmy Johnson. Doug bragged about being the only white kid in a band with two blacks and two Mexicans, as Hispanic youths in Texas were called back then. Kids above and below the legal drinking age of twenty-one crowded into the Tiffany for nightly dance parties, and for Doug the gigs spawned a reckoning about the direction he wanted his life to take. "I was playing sports in junior high," he would exaggerate (for school photos showed him in the marching band), "and I realized that the whole thing of going to school and getting your head busted playing football and all that shit wasn't it. I was playing all them great Fats Domino tunes at night, and I decided that's what I wanted to do . . . that's what really started changing my life."

Doug's parents doubtless heaved a sigh of relief when he graduated from Sam Houston High in 1958, but there was no question of his following his brother's example and going on to college. The musician's life had him firmly in its grip by then; he was out all night, playing gigs and chasing the pleasures that might follow. He played with rock-and-roll bands that competed for coveted "base gigs"—NCO and officers' club shows on the several air force bases and army posts in the city. One Chicano army sergeant who booked bands at a club called the Snake Pit would reward bands that could play his beloved blues, polkas, and cha-cha-cha. One time Doug shared a bill with an airman on one of the bases named Gene Pitney—the high-voiced singer with a string of hits that included "The Man Who Shot Liberty Valance" and "Town without Pity." Doug was more impressed when he played bills with Freddy Fender.

That hit singer was born Baldemar Huerta in the Rio Grande Valley town of San Benito in 1935. As he later told the story to National Public Radio's Terry Gross, his father died in the last year of World War II, leaving the family in hunger, barely sleeping under a roof. Baldemar's mother married a migrant farmworker, and the stepfather's life of working with his hands and a stooped back was passed on to the boy—to escape if he could. Between the harvest seasons disk jockeys of small stations along the Texas-Mexico border were delighted to discover a little boy from their culture who could sing. He caught on in a small way in South Texas and Mexico as "El Bebop Kid" with Spanish-language covers of Elvis's "Don't Be Cruel" and Harry Belafonte's "Jamaica Farewell."

His first manager, who drove a route of bars and cafés stocking jukeboxes, noted that he had sideburns and told him to find a name that would be remembered by gringos and would fit neatly on the label of a 45. He got the name Fender from the brand of his guitar and amplifier and picked Freddy with

an ear for alliteration. Though he signed with Fats Domino's label and was known as "the Mexican Elvis," he was still picking onions in Las Cruces, New Mexico, just a year before he played that gig with Doug and scored a minor national hit with his blues shuffle "Wasted Days and Wasted Nights." Doug was awed by what Fender could do with his voice, and the squealing of young girls filled him with pleasure, envy, and ambition. Then police found two joints of marijuana in Fender's apartment in Baton Rouge, and a judge sentenced him to three years in Louisiana's ferocious Angola prison.

By then Doug had established himself as an instrumentalist and club performer, but he wanted his own recordings with a bullet on the charts of

Doug playing with Rudy Grayzell and the Ah-Ha Cowboys during his short-lived rockabilly phase. Photo courtesy of Shawn Sahm.

Billboard, he wanted people hearing his voice on the radio, he wanted it all. Texas's first true rock-and-roll star was Buddy Holly—it's stark to remember that his run as a recording artist lasted just a year and a half before he was killed in the plane crash in Iowa. Roy Orbison came out of bleak oil towns along the Texas–New Mexico border with a strangely lovely quavering high voice during the same period. The elaborations of Holly and Orbison on rockabilly were not Doug's style, though he had great respect for them; he was influenced more by a succession of rhythm-and-blues artists. But the stars of rock and roll were not just the singers. Success was measured and driven by what got played on the radio, and apprentice musicians like Doug were influenced as much by disk jockeys as by their peers. The king of those was a Brooklyn-born man named Robert Weston Smith who had once gotten a cross burned in his yard by the Ku Klux Klan when he was playing rhythm-and-blues records and making irreverent cracks at a station in Shreveport. Now, with 250,000 watts of power at a station called XERF in the dusty border town of Ciudad Acuña, as Wolfman Jack he howled in imitation of black radio legends like Dr. Jive and Sugar Daddy and electrified listeners all across the American plains and southern forests.

Doug recorded singles for small labels in San Antonio called Satin, Warrior, Harlem, and Cobra. All were the creations of a former professional wrestler from the Kansas City area named Ed Hehnke. Disk jockeys at the local AM stations knew the top bands in town, and if they liked what they heard, they gladly pushed locally recorded singles into rotation with the national hits. Backed up by the Knights and boosted by this airplay, Doug chased the alchemy of radio hits in a revved-up imitation of Little Richard: "*Crazy crazy Daisy, why don't you treat your daddy right?*"

Moving to a Houston-based label, Renner, Doug had a regional hit in 1960 called "Why Why Why" that showcased his reverence for rhythm and blues and enlisted some of San Antonio's best young horn players. "His look in those days was a pompadour haircut, suit and tie, and a diamond pinkie ring," said Harvey Kagan, a bass player who first got to know him when Doug played with Harvey's brother, a lead guitarist, in a band called the Starmarks. Even at age nineteen Doug had a knack for identifying promising bands or players and providing tips and introductions to help them along, and he liked what he heard from Harvey Kagan. "I was a few years younger and kind of awed by him, because his songs were on the radio all the time, and he could play all these instruments, and play them so well."

Inspired by the success of "Why Why Why"—which earned a brief mention in *Billboard*—Doug hit the road for the first time in a used Oldsmobile, calling without much luck on club owners and booking and recording agents in Los Angeles, Chicago, and New York. When he came back to San Antonio he put together a nine-piece band propelled by Chicano sax and trumpet players—members of the loose collective that came to be known as the West Side Horns. One of those, a tenor sax player named Rocky Morales, became a fixture in Doug's bands anytime he decided he wanted a horn section.

Doug was an up-and-coming cool young cat, but San Antonio's top bandleader then was a black sax player, Spot Barnett, whose East Side base was the Club Ebony. Doug said, "He was the king—[he had] five old ladies, twenty-something kids, and the finest bands, with three players on horns . . . we were in the clubs, seeing Spot. We'd walk in and say, 'We got a band here.' The black cats would say, 'Oh, man, you bunch of honkies. Can you play that guitar? Let's see what you can do.' And I'd say, 'What you want to hear?' and then we'd hit it with 'Further On Up the Road,' or something like that. They'd invite us back and kind of took me under their wing."

Doug joined Barnett's band for a while, playing bass, and with their stand-out backing he got to record a sock-hop snuggler, "Just a Moment," as another A-side single in 1960. Doug thought he was singing like Junior Parker, but his voice broke on the sexiest part, and he tried to draw four or five syllables out of "moment"—he could play anything he got his hands on, but he was still a garage-band singer who hadn't figured out what to do with vowels.

———

The week before Christmas in 1961 Doug got as high as number 13 on the KONO chart with another slow-dance love song, "Crazy, Crazy Feeling," and a flip side, "Baby, What's on Your Mind," that with some maturing of his vocals and with thumping bass and lead guitar flair honored his heroes of big-city rhythm and blues. He brought back his West Side friends and horn players and returned to the local charts the following spring with a self-assured big band sound and some Tex-Mex rhythms. "Two Hearts in Love" was more teen pop, but couples crowded the dance floors and raised some steam with that one.

"Violet Morris," said Kagan, "had a job as an executive secretary in a Montgomery Ward's store in one of the shopping centers. Doug got some of us together to play a staff Christmas party, and that's where he and Violet got each other's attention." Violet was an attractive brunette and a divorced single mother of three small children. She said later that on first meeting Doug she had been a little put off by his hipster slang, but then she reminisced: "He was so pretty then. His hair had to be fixed Frankie Avalon–style, and he'd make me move over if I got too close and wrinkled his suit." They married in 1963, and he took on the responsibility of three stepchildren named Ron, Ginger, and Tammy. That same year Violet gave birth to their daughter Dawn. "The draft board was after me, they were on my tail," Doug would say, but at twenty-two, in taking on responsibility for a marriage and four small children,

Doug serenading his bride Violet.
Photo courtesy of Shawn Sahm.

he got himself classified 1-Y and had no worries about the draft in the turbulent years to come. He found them a rent house out in the country and scored a gig four nights a week at another small lounge called the Blue Note. He played there almost two years. "You just dug in," he said. "In the San Antonio clubs there was nothing but hustlers, pimps, strippers, and a few straggly flat-topped cats from Lackland"—a local air force base. "There weren't any hippies."

Doug would explain how rock and roll had come in with a blast in 1955 with Elvis, Little Richard, Fats Domino, Jerry Lee Lewis, and others who got their early breaks in Memphis and New Orleans. Then there was a lull, with the charts claimed by show-off novelty acts like the Coasters and slick singers like Frankie Avalon and Bobby Vinton. "Then in 1964," said Doug, "boy, here it came again. It was just four guys writing great songs and doing great harmonies in England."

Doug's friend Augie Meyers meanwhile played keyboards in a popular teen dance band called Denny Ezba and the Goldens. The bass player was Harvey Kagan. When the British wave hit San Antonio, Augie spotted the Vox electric organ, which had been introduced most notably by Alan Price in the Animals' "The House of the Rising Sun." Augie claimed that for $265 he bought the first Vox seen in an American band. He said he was initially entranced more by its look, the alternating black and white keys, than by the throbbing sounds Price and other English players coaxed out of it. The boyhood polio victim was now a tall, imposing, rawboned young married man with a powerful-looking jaw. He

Doug as the hometown soul singer and band leader. Photo courtesy of Shawn Sahm.

was one of the first in their crowd of musicians who started growing his hair down over his ears, and if anybody objected, well, what of it?

During those months Doug abruptly grew out of his vocal conceits and turned in his most confident singing in "Mr. Kool" and "Son of Bill Baety"—the latter a wonderfully phrased tale by Leadbelly in the barroom shootout vein of "Frankie and Johnny." But then Doug's Houston label dropped him, and he turned to pestering the top record producer in Texas, Huey P. Meaux, the self-styled "Crazy Cajun." At first the San Antonio youth got nowhere. Meaux had spent his early childhood years living on his dad's sharecrop farm near Lafayette, Louisiana. As a child he spoke mostly Cajun French. His dad played accordion in a Cajun band, calling himself Pappy Te-Tan, and Huey was, he said later, a very poor drummer in the band. The family moved across the Texas border to a little town called Winnie when the boy was twelve. Huey's local contemporaries included the country singer George Jones and J. P. Richardson, a disk jockey who as "The Big Bopper" recorded a novelty hit called "Chantilly Lace" and died in the plane crash that claimed Buddy Holly and Ritchie Valens. Huey came of age cutting hair in a Winnie barbershop and spinning records at a local radio station, KPAC, and at teen parties. He edged into producing bands with names like Jivin' Gene and the Jokers and Big Sambo and the Housebreakers.

A swampy forest in the southeast corner of Texas was called the Golden Triangle because of rich oil discoveries, among them 1901's Spindletop. Refineries blazed natural gas flares at night over ports filled with tankers and shrimp boats. Janis Joplin and the brothers Johnny and Edgar Winter were among the native talents who grew up and got out of those towns as fast as they could, but the Golden Triangle was the creative and entrepreneurial turf of Huey P. Meaux. (He tried to market the Winter brothers as an act called the Great Believers; they got nowhere, he inferred, because people in those swamps were easily spooked by one white albino guitar player, let alone by two.) Meaux was notorious for buying songs from writers for fifty bucks, and in large type he then claimed he was the songwriter when he pressed the Tribe vinyls. He was acquisitive and sharp enough in this backroom trade that, according to journalist Joe Nick Patoski, he wound up owning "Babalu," Desi Arnaz's dance-band sensation in pre-Castro Cuba. He relieved a Gulfport, Mississippi, songwriter named Jimmy Donley of a number of sappy love songs like "Please, Mr. Sandman." One day Donley called Meaux up to thank him for all that he'd done for the songsmith and his career over the years; forty-five minutes later Donley committed suicide.

Meaux was a phenomenal hustler and an outlandish character, and he knew his music. He made his early mark recording rhythm and blues and zydeco, the French patois blues born of Cajun juke joints. The sound most strongly identified with his records created its own genre called "swamp pop." He recorded artists as successful as Big Mama Thornton, Clifton Chenier, and Lightnin' Hopkins, and he sent a smooth-faced young singer named Sunny Azuna and his band the Sunlighters to break through the ethnic barricade of *American Bandstand* with a cover of Little Willie John's "Talk to Me" in 1962.

In Beaumont Meaux discovered a teen guitarist and singer named Barbara Lynn and convinced her parents to let him sign her and record "If You Lose Me, You'll Lose a Good Thing" in 1963. The profits from that hit enabled Meaux to move his base of operations to Houston. And Meaux already had a pair of able white singers from Texas: Three Rivers' Roy Head, on his way to a gold record with "Treat Her Right," and Rosenberg's B. J. Thomas, whose hit was a smooth and sexy cover of Hank Williams's "So Lonesome I Could Cry."

"Huey would hold court in his barbershop in Winnie, a little town between Beaumont and Port Arthur," Doug recalled, "and if you were a young guy trying to get a national hit, you had to go see him there. He had this box of 45s beside the barber's chair, clippings of hair all over it. He'd take out a record, dust the hair off, and tell you, 'Go listen to this and come back in six months.'"

Whatever Huey P. Meaux thought of the potential of the supercharged young man, he had his own problems at the time—swamp pop and his Tribe label were being washed off the charts by the English tidal wave. There are two versions of how Huey's fit of nerves culminated in a band. Meaux claimed that he carried some Beatles and other records and a little turntable to San Antonio and rented three rooms in a motel. The stakes, he said, were nothing less than whether he could master the music business or quit. He went on that he was playing his dad's recording of "Lake Charles Two-Step," and it came to him that the Beatles were doing the same thing: "The beat was *on the beat,* just like a Cajun two-step."

Meaux said he then called Doug and urged him to come to the motel but warned him he should stay away if he was going to be judgmental, because he'd been deep in that Thunderbird for days and was badly messed up. Meaux said he told him he had to start growing his hair long, and then told him to tune out the accordion and listen to the beat of the Cajun song. Meaux said Doug solved the puzzle of the Beatles' harmonies by listening to those on "Big Mamou" and others by one of his heroes, the Houston Cajun blues singer Papa Link Davis.

Others didn't remember it quite that way. In the recollection of Augie Meyers and Harvey Kagan, Huey P.'s reveries wouldn't have done anyone immediate good if a successful English knockoff of the Beatles, the Dave Clark Five, hadn't come to San Antonio for a concert in 1964 without some essential baggage. Opening acts for the concert were Denny Ezba and the Goldens and Doug and the Mar-Kays. When roadies discovered that the Brits had somehow arrived without the Vox organ played by lead singer Mike Smith, a frantic scramble ensued. Augie's loan of his instrument rescued the headline act. And Meaux was out in the crowd, taking the measure of Doug and Augie.

Maybe the truth has room for both versions. Kagan said, "After that Huey got Doug and Augie working together. Doug had his band, and Augie was playing with Denny Ezba and the Goldens. They were doing this thing with Huey on the side, very quietly, and none of us knew anything about it. Denny could not believe it when Augie told him he was quitting the band to join up with Doug." Other members of the new group, the drummer Johnny Perez and bass player Jack Barber, were already playing with Doug's band. "At first we had a black saxophone and maracas player," Augie said, "but it was a problem for him anytime we had to go anywhere and check in a hotel or go to a restaurant, so he quit and we hired Frank Morin," who was Hispanic.

In naming the band the Sir Douglas Quintet, Doug left no doubt that he was the group's driving force; his ego compelled him to be the bandleader, whomever he played with, the rest of his life. In their first single the Quintet tried to extract the Beatles' magic from a cover of "Sugar Bee," a song written by Cleveland Crochet, a fiddler with a band called the Hillbilly Ramblers, that in 1961 had been the first Cajun hit to make the *Billboard* Top 100. The youths' rock-and-roll version generated no such response.

But they were playing a gig one night, getting their chops down, and a dancer in front of the stage was putting on a show, tossing her skirt as she twirled and pranced. Doug leaned away from the microphone and said to the others with a grin, "She's a body mover, isn't she?" And that was the song title at first—"She's a Body Mover." But Huey and others raised objections that it was just too sexy and suggestive; the disk jockeys would never play it. So the title evolved into "She's About a Mover." The song was short, just under two and a half minutes—which was largely Doug's career-long, pop-conscious style.

It began with chords of Doug's guitar, then a banging of a tambourine, and then the exotic entry of Augie's Vox. He played it with an insistent pumping of two- and three-note bursts that were almost an echo of how he grew up hearing the accordion, and later learned to play it. Doug held the Cajun music of south Louisiana in high regard, but he agreed with Augie that they got it from their own ethnic and cultural roots. They jumped up the tempo of what they'd first heard as Tex-Mex German-Polish-Czech dance music. "Oom-pah-pah came first," Augie contended. "'She's About a Mover,' that's just a polka with a rock-and-roll beat."

"Well, she was walking down the street / looking fine as she could be." Two lyrical couplets about a brassy girl and cool guy told scarcely more story than that. Overdubbing was rare in those days, but Doug added the backup tracks and was the only singer. He repeated the hook line ten times. The second-most-repeated line was a none-too-subtle borrowing from "What'd I Say," a big hit by one Ray Charles. Doug was a versatile songwriter, but he usually stayed away from lyrics with a complex narrative; he wanted people going around singing two or three lines that they'd heard on the radio and couldn't get out of their heads. With this song he'd done it. Augie and the Crazy Cajun could go on debating what the players did with the beat, but on the radio the sound was as irresistible as the sound of a small-town carnival: what it really seemed to race with and echo was the listener's pulse.

clockwise: Family snapshot of Doug in uniform of junior high band. Doug strikes a rare church-going pose while in his early teens (1955). Doug's high school graduation portrait. Photos courtesy of Shawn Sahm.

Song and Dance Men

They recorded at the *Gold Star Studios* in Houston in January 1965. (When Meaux later prospered enough to buy the studio, he changed the name to SugarHill.) According to Meaux, "She's About a Mover" first broke out on a Port Arthur station, KPAC; it became a sensation first in Louisiana, then came back across the Sabine to Texas. Meaux licensed the record abroad to the London-American label and told the musicians to keep their mouths shut until he got the record on the national charts. Meaux had an overbearing sense of marketing—he wouldn't let the band do anything to promote the record until he was certain the time was right. "One night we had a gig in San Antonio," Doug recalled, "and this guy came up and said, 'What are you doing? You've got a song that's number one from Houston to Miami, and you're in this dump with two hundred people!'"

By April "She's About a Mover" was streaking up the charts on both sides of the Atlantic, peaking in the United States at number 13. Huey outfitted them in black Beatle suits and boots and got them on bills with the Rolling Stones, James Brown, the Beach Boys, and Little Richard, and he told them just to sing—not to say anything. The ruse couldn't work very long, but for a short time radio jocks and listeners thought they really *were* British.

Doug laughed, "I'd say 'Pip pip' and stuff like that when we met Peter Townshend and the Who, while trying to hush Johnny and Frank, who'd be going, 'Hey, qué pasó?' What's happening?"

According to Augie, Meaux required married band members to take off their wedding rings before a performance; the young girls who were the target audience needed to believe, or at least fantasize, that the musicians were *available*. The promotional climax came with appearances on *American Bandstand* and the prime-time music program *Hullabaloo*. Sponsored by brands of toothpaste and car wax, and a deodorant that provided "gentle protection without harshness," the *Hullabaloo* show began with a well-scrubbed crew of dancers with V-neck sweaters, modestly short skirts, and go-go boots. There was a lot of hair-shaking as an announcer introduced Chuck Berry, grinning and snapping his fingers, Vickie Carr, the Four Seasons, Freddie and the Dreamers, Herman's Hermits, Martha and the Vandellas, and finally the lads from San Antonio. But the newcomers could not complain about their positioning. Holding a guitar and wearing a business suit, white shirt, and tie, the host was Trini Lopez, a Dallas native who was known mostly for his version of the folk song "If I Had a Hammer." Lopez said it was his pleasure to introduce royalty: "Ladies and gentlemen, lords and ladies, the Sir Douglas Quintet."

In the first number of the show, they appeared in front of a set of boards cut and painted to resemble English castles. Another prop was an armored knight riding a horse and carrying a jousting lance. A young woman with a breastplate of armor was assigned to move not a muscle, barely an eyelash, as the musicians carried on about a street girl and boogied, kicking their Beatle boots in periodic tandem. Was she meant to be a princess? Joan of Arc? Whatever role she was told to play, she was no body mover. The strange choreography didn't matter, for the song's jumpy beat and Doug's cocksure singing got the program racing. Doug looked like he might have been at home on the streets of Liverpool or London. He had gotten his nose broken somewhere along the line, and as a lower-middle-class kid he had grown up without the benefit of braces on his teeth.

But the most striking thing about Doug was his hair. It really wasn't that long, but it appeared that Doug's wife or perhaps the bass player Jack Barber, who really was a barber, had set in whacking with scissors. The kid who had tried to dress up like Frankie Avalon was transformed into a tough guy—strong jaw, a face composed of craggy angles, interesting. Barber, Morin, and Perez went through the routine stone-faced, but a viewer who saw that number would never have guessed that Augie had a handicap from his childhood polio. He was dancing behind the Vox and—pay attention, England—shaking his hair like a dust mop.

When they hit the last notes and finished their wiggles and kicks, Lopez walked out briskly. "I suppose all you folks assume these fellows are from England," he said, grinning. "But I have a surprise for you. They're from my home state of Texas—can you believe it?"

Doug stepped forward again and slyly drawled into the camera, "Y'all come back. Heahh?"

Unlike other stars, Doug was not yet inclined to put his guitar down, grab a microphone, and sing without an instrument, but he was learning that he could free up his hands and let the band play on as he snaked his arms and scooted about the stage in his evolving routine. He loved being a showman. The Quintet also got to show off their moves on ABC's *Shindig!* and a Dick Clark production, *Where the Action Is.* "One time," Augie told me, "Huey called us and said he had us on with the Monkees. We had to get up early in the morning in North Dakota and fly to Minnesota, and then Chicago, and then to Ohio and Virginia and Philadelphia, changing planes every stop. We got to Maryland at seven in the evening and this guy says, 'You're on next. You've got four songs.'" They embarked on a tour of Europe, a rarity in those days. It was hard and thrilling work.

The soaring highs were matched by crushing lows. One night back in Texas Violet Sahm had a frightening dream—there was an airplane, and in it Doug was in a coffin. Violet's premonition was just off, in the way of dreams. The band was in Chicago for a concert when the call came that Doug's dad had died of a heart attack. The airplane carried him home to San Antonio, but he had little time to grieve and console his mother before boarding another flight to rejoin the band.

The Quintet was not the only Texas rock band that broke out in 1965. For years public confusion of one of them with the Quintet saddled the Quintet's leader with the mispronunciation of his name as Doug *Sham.* But Doug admired the gall and jive of Domingo Samudio, a Chicano from the Dallas area who had once played in a garage band with Trini Lopez and then moved to Memphis and became the turban-wearing showman of Sam the Sham and the Pharaohs. They scored big national hits that year with "Wooly Bully" and "Little Red Riding Hood." Their music featured a *dink-dink-dink* organ that sounded much like Augie's Vox. Also in 1965, a Bay City, Michigan, Mexican American group who called themselves Question Mark and the Mysterians used a strikingly similar Vox lead to propel a garage-band classic, "96 Tears."

The Quintet encountered unexpected difficulty in following up on their first hit. Their next release, "The Tracker," sounded so much like "She's About a Mover" that disk jockeys declined to play it. "Also," Augie said, "they listened to it and thought Doug was calling himself a *tractor*." Doug had tried being a screamer on a corny song about a lover who enlisted the CIA and a fleet of submarines to help chase down his honey; the low point was when he yelled, "Yeah, blow your horns"—next in the arrangement was a solo by Augie on his Vox. That was typical Doug Sahm, both in his studio ebullience and his resistance to editing. Another release, "In Time," was a stretch. Both in Augie's organ play and the harmonizing behind Doug's lead, it seemed they were trying too hard to sound like the Animals.

But in the Houston studio under Huey Meaux's watchful eye they celebrated an astonishing array of music: Leadbelly's scary blues song "In the Pines," in which a man cuts off a rival lover's head and makes sure the rest of his body is never found; "It's a Man Down There," bluesman G. L. Crockett's tweaks of Sonny Boy Williamson's "One Way Out," which the Allman Brothers later made one of their anthems; and covers of several country songs, including a riotous take on Jimmie Rodgers's "In the Jailhouse Now." They regained the charts later that year when Huey steered them back to the well. In a raggedly typed letter to an interviewer during one of his subsequent prison terms, Meaux claimed he wrote the Quintet's next hit in a truck stop during a drive back home from New Orleans: "My girlfriend had left me and I was down about that. It was 3 a.m. in the morning I remember it was raining cats and dogs. I wanted to get me some black coffee so I could make it to Winnie before I fell asleep. This truck driver came in and stomped his boots and had a brown corduroy cap and slapped it against his leg and said *This is the day that the rains came*." And so, Meaux claimed, he wrote "The Rains Came" on a paper napkin.

Another story about the song's provenance was that Meaux had bought the rights for twenty-five dollars from Big Sambo Young and made it a swamp pop hit on the Tribe label by Big Sambo and the Housebreakers. Doug said on one recorded occasion that one stormy night he wrote it in New Braunfels in tribute to a special woman friend. However it came about, Meaux claimed songwriting credit on the record and got that substantial chunk of change from the royalties. With the backup singers delightfully off-key, the secrets were Augie's carnylike organ and Doug giving soulful voice to lyrics that were so simple they almost belied the term. "*Rain rain rain rain . . .*" Dick Clark booked them on *American Bandstand* to perform both of their hits, and this time Doug's costume featured a cowboy hat.

Elvis Presley lost the magic of the Memphis and Sun Records days when he was drafted and came out of the army acting in bad movies. American pop music's only real answer to the Beatles, the Stones, and the other English stars was Bob Dylan. The writer with the acoustic guitar, harmonica, and odd singing voice had shucked his folk trappings and surrounded himself with superb rock musicians, most of whom were Canadians; they then called themselves the Hawks and later became the Band. Divided into A and B sides for the convenience of disk jockeys who were hanging on to the old ways of Top 40 AM radio, Dylan's epic song "Like a Rolling Stone" vaulted to the top of the charts, yet just about everywhere he went Dylan and his players were booed by fans who thought he'd sold out. The first place they played electric and weren't booed was in Austin, Texas. At the end of the year they had scheduled five dates in ten days in the San Francisco area. In December 1965 Dylan consented to a televised press conference in San Francisco—the only time he ever did that. The crowd of reporters clearly had no idea what to make of this unusual young man, or what to ask him. Seated at a table, Dylan chain-smoked cigarettes and fended them off with smiles and wisecracks.

One man said, "Are you a singer or a poet?"

"I think of myself as a song and dance man, you know."

Another reporter asked if he was trying to punish old girlfriends or woo them back in songs such as "Like a Rolling Stone," which had been widely interpreted as misogynistic. He blew another stream of smoke and laughed.

"I needle them."

"If you were going to sell out to a commercial interest, which one would you choose?"

"Ladies' garments."

One of the reporters asked him if he could recommend any up-and-coming bands with commercial prospects. "Oh, great, I'm glad you asked that. I think the Sir Douglas Quintet is the best band that has a chance to reach commercial airwaves. They already have with a couple of songs."

———

An unsolicited public endorsement of the Quintet's music by Bob Dylan! Reporters scrambled to find out who these guys were and locate their records. How did that happen? Years later, Doug described their meeting in New York in 1965 in an interview by John Swenson that was published by *Crawdaddy,* a prominent rock magazine. As it often happened to Doug, Swenson rendered his speech as redneck dialect. The story was titled "The Psychedelic Cowboy Makes His Move."

"Aw, it was jes destiny y'know. The first tahm ah actually saw him was at the Kettle of Fish with Brian Jones an' it was really a trip. That was th' first tahm we'd come to th' city, we were really hicks in them days, man, jes out from th' woods. It seems lahk that everbody, y'know, man, he did such a thing to that era with that role that he played, that lil monster lil magic guy with th' words an' y'know that whole trip, that aura . . ."

Rock-and-roll writers might think he talked like an incoherent hayseed, but the bottom line was that in little more than a year he'd gone from opening for the Dave Clark Five in San Antonio to hanging out in New York with Dylan and the Rolling Stones guitarist Brian Jones. In one of the prison letters Huey Meaux added another twist to the Quintet's tale. "The album came out late because I had hell getting Doug back from England. He ran into Bob Dylan there and could buy pot in the drug store like you did cigs. . . . Augie was the brain behind the business part. Doug hated it, so I talked to Augie when I wanted things done . . . Augie Meyers is a good man."

That letter contained a broad hint that Meaux added to the rivalry that always spiced and complicated the friendship of Doug and Augie. But all the Quintet's members were heroes to youths in San Antonio. Radio KONO's Top 100 chart for 1965 had their song at number 4; the three above it were all products of British bands, with the Stones' "Satisfaction" at number 1. The Quintet were full-blown rock stars, famous throughout North America and Europe, which naturally led to their arrests for marijuana possession in Corpus Christi two days before their year of huge success came to an end.

It was a planned and orchestrated bust. Doug and Frank Morin flew down to play a gig but were greeted in the airport by plainclothesmen who curtly told them to behave themselves and come along. Augie had driven down that morning with Jack Barber. "I was gassing up my car that morning, and I noticed this white car. I kept noticing it, and then when we got down to Corpus, they pulled us over, and all of a sudden I was looking at a rifle pointed at my face. The head of that operation was a frustrated guitar player. They had just busted [country singer] Ray Price and his band." Johnny Perez had ridden down in the prized '36 hot rod Ford of Charlie Pritchard, who was just along for the fun of it. Pritchard was a guitarist who knew the band from his hometown of San Antonio and was then living and playing in Austin with a top band called the Conqueroo. Pritchard had been scheduled to play at a benefit for an ailing black fiddler in Austin; it was the only time Janis Joplin ever appeared with the pioneering psychedelic band the 13th Floor Elevators. Pritchard recalled that when he protested the confiscation of his prized car over a couple of grams of pot, the cops chortled, "You're lucky to get out of here with your ass. We haven't had as much fun since we confiscated Ray Price's bus."

The *Corpus Christi Times* jeered the musicians the next morning with the headline "Musicians Face the Music—La(w) La(w)." Though they turned their faces away from television cameras when they were released from the city jail, the paper claimed that Doug at first made a face at the reporters, then ran his fingers through his hair and popped off, "Give us a guitar if you want us to perform."

But it was no joking matter. Earlier that year Violet had given birth to their first son Shawn; at twenty-four Doug was now responsible for the welfare of five small children. And this being Texas, where sentences of twenty years or more were routinely handed down for convictions of marijuana possession, he and his companions were in danger of serious prison time.

Doug later told his children how he strutted into his lawyer's office and proceeded to lay out his credentials as a rock-and-roll star who was high up in

the entertainment business and was known and valued all over the world. The
lawyer let him vent and spew, nodded, then said, "What's gonna happen here
is you're gonna stop talking, you're gonna start listening, and you're gonna get
the kind of haircut that attracts no attention, and if you do what you're told you
might avoid sitting on your ass in prison for the next decade or two." Doug was
next seen in a brown suit, white shirt, and plain brown tie, with his short oiled
hair combed back over his ears—he looked like a young insurance adjuster.
The victims of the bust avoided jail time with respectable juvenile records
and some hard-bought lawyers. Perhaps because Doug's arrest occurred in
an airport, his case wound up under the jurisdiction of a federal court, whose
magistrates were not so fond of imposing long, harsh sentences for drug viola-
tions. They all got off with five years' probation, but unlike Doug, Augie was
forbidden to leave the state for those years. The legal system's control of the
musicians' lives thwarted Huey Meaux's frantic efforts to keep them afloat in
the charts. He rushed out an album called *The Best of the Sir Douglas Quintet,*
which was fair enough an assessment of the songs they had in the Tribe label's
can, but it implied they had been around for several years. In the perception of
many Texans the Quintet went from being an entertaining band with a clever
gimmick to being rock-and-roll outlaws. And since the photo Meaux selected
for the cover of the LP cast them in unrecognizable shadows, it soon came to
the players' attention that while their opportunity dried up, groups all over the
United States and Canada were offering themselves in gigs as the Sir Douglas
Quintet.

They wound up playing gigs in Texas backwaters. A small-college fraternity put
on one such dance in a low-ceilinged hall called the MB Corral in Wichita Falls,
near the Oklahoma border. I was a member of that fraternity; we had been
kicked off campus for some shameful deed and as first-time rock promoters
were trying to recover our finances and reputations. Our first choice was the
rockabilly band the Bobby Fuller Four, an ultimate one-hit wonder; we learned
that the Texas-born Fuller, who had gotten up to number 4 on the charts with
"I Fought the Law," had died in California, officially ruled a suicide but more
likely a murder victim. We were astonished by how much money these groups
commanded for playing a couple of hours. The Sir Douglas Quintet was the
biggest name we could get with our money in hand.

The MB Corral, where they played the show, belonged to members of a western swing band called the Miller Brothers, one of whom, the trumpet player, had been my next-door neighbor when I was growing up. Most evenings the MB was a country honky-tonk, but on off Thursday and Sunday nights they rented the place to black promoters who brought in some of the same blues bands that electrified the Eastwood Country Club in San Antonio. In an enhancement of a local street legend, a *Rolling Stone* writer named Grover Lewis would give the MB Corral a measure of national ill repute by claiming that one night he and his novelist friend Larry McMurtry "stood among a circle of spectators in the parking lot one drizzly night and watched a nameless oilfield worker batter and kick Elvis Presley half to death in what was delicately alluded to afterwards as a difference of opinion about the availability of the roughneck's girlfriend."

Things did not go that badly for Sir Doug and the band at the MB Corral. They were duded up in their black Beatle suits and boots and put on an energetic and disciplined show. But cops swarmed around the MB that evening. The youths packed inside the hall were forbidden any alcohol, even those who were of legal age to buy it—but they made do. Doug later remarked that he'd never seen so much glue-sniffing in his life. When gigs like that were finished and they had gotten paid, they didn't linger and pal around with the folks who hired them. "Damn, there's some mean towns out there," said Augie, recalling that period in their lives.

Doug could not bear being locked into that dreary routine. He used the slack time to get a plastic surgeon to straighten his nose. Then, as soon as his probation officer assured him he would not be reported a fugitive, he loaded up his family and took off for California, the much friendlier golden land.

Doug with college students during "Mendocino" success (1968 or '69). Photo courtesy of Ron Oberman.

Summers of Love

oug settled his family not in San Francisco, where outlying roads were littered with broken-down Volkswagens of hippies trying to make the trip, but in the blue-collar Salinas Valley suburb of Prunedale. With his share of the Quintet proceeds he and Violet bought a spacious tract house that sat on a few acres amid towering stands of eucalyptus trees. About an hour's drive south from San Francisco, it was the country on the curve of Monterey Bay that gained fame through the novels of John Steinbeck. Their neighbors included factory workers and day-labor field hands. But at the same time Doug played an integral role in the frolic and havoc centered in Haight-Ashbury, the once-genteel neighborhood adjoining Golden Gate Park.

If you were young and rebellious, between May 1965 and June 1966 San Francisco was the most exciting place on earth. During those extraordinary months the Rolling Stones debuted at the Civic Auditorium, and the Beatles set off a crowd stampede at the Cow Palace; the Warlocks changed their name to the Grateful Dead for a concert produced by Bill Graham at the Fillmore Auditorium; the California attorney general decried the widespread legal use of LSD to a legislative judiciary committee in Sacramento; Lenny Bruce, Lou Reed and the Velvet Underground, and Andy Warhol and His Plastic Inevitable shared Fillmore bills with Frank Zappa and the Mothers of Invention; the Fugs, Country Joe and the Fish, the Paul Butterfield Blues Band, and Ken Kesey and His Merry Pranksters also stirred the counterculture's stew. Doug Sahm not only fit in—he thrived and seemed to be everywhere at once.

He drove Bill Graham wild by showing up at the Fillmore Auditorium with thirteen musicians in the band when Graham had stipulated he could only bring five. Roaming the city in a cowboy hat and boots and the kind of duster one saw in movies about Jesse James or Wyatt Earp, he sauntered into the office of the new *Rolling Stone* magazine one day for what writers thought would be an editorial meeting. He popped open his briefcase and started showing them carefully wrapped varieties of choice Mexican marijuana. "Doug had girlfriends staked out in apartments all over the city," laughed his friend, the rock historian and critic Joel Selvin, "and he had that family scene with his wife and kids out in Prunedale."

Frank Morin and Johnny Perez followed the Quintet's leader to California, but Augie Meyers and Jack Barber stayed behind. "Doug kept calling me and telling me to come out," Augie told the story. "But at first my probation officer said I couldn't leave Texas. I was married and had a family myself, a boy in school. Clay came home one day and said their new teacher told them he used to be a policeman. They asked him what he ever did, who he'd put in jail, and he told them, 'Well, I helped arrest the Sir Douglas Quintet.'"

There were still some outstanding Sir Douglas Quintet obligations afloat in Texas and on the road. Augie got Harvey Kagan and three other San Antonio musicians to help honor those commitments. "One time we were doing this gig up in Canada, and this guy asked, 'How'd you get here?' Augie told him, 'We drove.' The guy said, 'Well, you must have really been flyin' low, because I saw the Sir Douglas Quintet yesterday in the Hollywood Bowl!'"

The San Antonio band might be splintered and scattered, but that didn't mean Doug was short of productive new friends. One of great importance hailed from El Paso originally, but he was reputed in San Francisco to be a full-blood Mexican Aztec, and he may have taken his name from an Argentine epic poem titled *Martin Fierro*. Whatever his tribe and heritage, Fierro formed a close bond with Doug in Northern California. They shared a passion for the very best in Mexican pot, and Fierro was a tremendous tenor sax player who had been playing with the fast-breaking psychedelic rock band Quicksilver Messenger Service.

The San Francisco music scene was then pretty small—everyone tended to know each other. Doug picked up the players he needed to make a band and continued to call it the Sir Douglas Quintet. In June 1966 the radio station KFRC put on a big Cow Palace concert headlined by the Beach Boys, the Byrds, Percy Sledge, the Lovin' Spoonful, and the Quintet in its San Francisco debut. The opening bands, Doug claimed, were the Jefferson Airplane and the Grateful Dead. "I remember telling [Jerry] Garcia, 'Hey, you're going to make it.' That's where our friendship began."

Another important figure in Doug's new life was an engineer named Dan Healy. A neighbor who played guitar for Quicksilver introduced him to Jerry Garcia, whose magnetic effect on people brought him into the orbit of the Grateful Dead in 1965. Healy would work with the band for years, creating as his legacy the legendary if impractical "Wall of Sound" performance system that weighed twenty tons and required twenty roadies to assemble onstage. Healy, whose parents were swing era jazz musicians living in a small Northern California town, connected with Doug just talking about music—so much of Doug's formative music was western swing, a regional variant of big band jazz, and Healy was further pleased that the southerner's taste in blues ran not to the solo acoustic vein of swampland juke joints, but to the polished and orchestrated form associated with Chicago. Through Healy's friendship with Garcia, Doug and the Quintet opened for the Dead in Oakland, with an enthusiastic crowd response, and they continued to pair up in gigs from time to time. During that period Healy went on a trip to Europe, and he was astonished to learn that the voices and instrumental sound of Sir Doug and the Quintet resounded on jukeboxes all over England and France.

Though many hippies gravitated to Graham's Fillmore, the center of the Texas expatriate activity was a downtown dance hall called the Avalon Ballroom. The upstairs room had a balcony, walls of mirrors, and the wildest light shows and poster art anyone had ever seen. Doug and the reformulated Quintet first played there in July 1966 (and by continuing to play the Avalon on a regular basis, likely sacrificed the possibility of more gigs at the Fillmore, for that was the kind of hardball Graham played). Founders of the Avalon were Chet Helms, whose Texas roots were in Fort Worth, and Travis Rivers, an Austin refugee who brought Janis Joplin from Port Arthur to San Francisco to sing for another Avalon house band, Big Brother and the Holding Company. For a few weeks, to the glee of disk jockeys who helped make a hit out of the 13th Floor Elevators' "You're Gonna Miss Me," the Austin band and their singer and lead guitarist, Roky Erickson, played the Avalon and other San Francisco venues in the fall of 1966. Erickson was so transported by acid during one Avalon gig that he turned his back on the audience the entire show and communicated with the feedback on his amplifier. Doug Sahm thought Erickson and the Elevators were riveting. Many pop historians credited the Elevators with inventing psychedelic rock, but they were too over-the-top for San Francisco tastes and too unreliable for managers of its venues; by the Christmas holidays they were back in Texas.

Other San Francisco émigrés from Texas included a pair of guitarists and singers who had struck up a friendship while attending a posh Dallas prep school, St. Mark's. Steve Miller's blues-rock band quickly became one of the regulars at the Avalon. His pal Boz Scaggs had been a member of a popular Austin band called the Wig (which featured longtime Austin stalwart Rusty Wier on drums). Scaggs moved on to Wisconsin, and then while traveling the world was proclaimed "the Bob Dylan of Sweden." Arriving in San Francisco with his air of maximum cool, he was discovered by *Rolling Stone* founder Jann Wenner. During this same period Johnny Winter, the white albino blues guitarist from Beaumont, won a whopping six-figure deal with Columbia Records because of a brief mention in the hot new San Francisco publication.

None of those acts could pull rank on the Sir Douglas Quintet in the Bay Area. In October 1966 the Quintet shared a memorable bill at the Avalon with Big Brother and the Holding Company and Janis Joplin, their doomed star from Texas. But despite their popularity, on radio station playlists and in record stores the Quintet hits were fast becoming golden oldies. Huey Meaux tried to fool disk jockeys by licensing Quintet recordings of "It's a Man Down There" under the pseudonym Him and "Wine Wine Wine" as the Devons. Under the Quintet name on the Tribe label they tried to follow up "The Rains Came" with a jarring remake of Gary U.S. Bonds' "A Quarter to Three"; then came another of Doug's attempts to make a hit out of a brokenhearted love song, "The Beginning of the End." The title was prophetic. Meaux could not effectively manage the band, the recordings, and the promotion from his base in Houston. In January 1967 they played in Golden Gate Park with the Grateful Dead, Big

Brother, and the Jefferson Airplane at the celebrated Gathering of the Tribes for a Human Be-In. Weeks later the California version of the band broke up.

The success of the Quintet had pulled the Crazy Cajun out of a perilous business nosedive, but now in the bewildering flux of FM rock he was having trouble getting any of his Tribe label records on the air. In October 1966 he attended a disk jockeys' convention in Nashville. In preparations for the trip he talked an eighteen-year-old boy who worked at a Houston radio station into enlisting a sixteen-year-old friend as a euphemistic "party girl" who might help him scare up some business. Huey paid her three hundred dollars for her effort. After the Nashville convention, the eighteen-year-old boy was arrested in Houston on drug charges. Federal investigators told the kid and his lawyer that the narcotics charges could go away if he would give up the Crazy Cajun. Huey Meaux was charged and convicted of conspiracy to violate the White Slave Traffic Act—otherwise known as the Mann Act—which makes it a federal crime to cross state lines to promote prostitution and other acts of moral turpitude. Huey had always been a flamboyant operator, but the case sent shock waves through the radio and record-selling communities in Texas. According to the U.S. Bureau of Prisons, he wound up serving eight months in a federal prison in Seagoville, Texas, in 1967. He later received a full pardon from President Jimmy Carter.

Meanwhile Augie and his wife and young son lived in a rented farmhouse in Bulverde, a little town in the hills northwest of San Antonio. He assembled an aspiring soul group with a wry and portentous name, Lord August and the Visions of Lite. The bass player was his pal from Denny Ezba and the Goldens, Harvey Kagan. Augie had loads of versatile talent, but he made his reputation as a sideman, an innovative player of the Vox organ. The appeal of the Vox was that it was cheaper and easier to haul around than the Hammond B-3, which had a huge wood cabinet and required several dollies to maneuver onstage. Another cheap import, the Farfisa from Italy, became popular with groups that subscribed to the garage band ethic. The sound Augie produced on the cheap organ came to be known as the Farfisa style of play, though he never changed brands. Sam the Sham and the Pharaohs and Question Mark and the Mysterians also used the roller rink sound to great advantage in their hits of 1965, and the style and sound were picked up and passed along over the years by Pink Floyd, Led Zeppelin, the B-52s, the Talking Heads, and Elvis Costello. But no one played the keyboard organ quite like Augie.

Weaving onstage like a snake charmer, he also played the accordion like he'd grown up hearing it in cantinas. Augie played rhythm guitar with steady prowess, sang with a pleasant drawling baritone voice, and developed a tremendous look. Wraps of thick black hair covered all of his ears and came together in a ropelike braid down the middle of his back that in time reached almost to his waist. This was joined to a thick-jawed beard and mustache worthy of a lumberjack. For a while he had been fitted with a plastic earpiece that veiled his minor birth defect, but during one gig it dropped off, making him so mad he kicked it into the astonished crowd. The persistent rumor that trailed him after he developed his trademark look was that he wore his hair that way because he had gotten an ear sliced off in a knife fight, and he carried his pickled ear from gig to gig in a glass jar as a morbid reminder how easily trouble could come his way.

Doug and Augie were very close friends, but their relationship always contained elements of pulling rank and jealous competition. Doug chided him as the king of tall tales and was always saying, "Don't let that ponytail fool you. He is 100 percent redneck underneath." But when Augie and Doug led a band onstage people gasped at the spectacle. Augie's mass of black hair and beard and the limp from his childhood polio stirred notions of a Hollywood pirate, and beside him strode Doug in his duster and cowboy hat.

"Too hot in here," Doug would complain.

"Well, take off your coat."

"No, they gotta get us a fan."

They were an exceptional team, and though they often pursued their dreams in separate bands, they knew how well they worked together, and they never lost the spark of friendship they had when they were teenagers in San Antonio breaking up bubble gum packages to get the baseball cards.

Lord August and the Visions of Lite recorded one little-noticed album; then they were working in Georgia on a movie with Otis Redding when the singer's plane crashed in a Wisconsin lake. Redding's death scuttled the project, and Augie was soon back in Texas, trying to land gigs and hold his band together. He talked for a while about going to Las Vegas and leading an act in the casinos. At that point in their lives he needed Doug worse than Doug needed him.

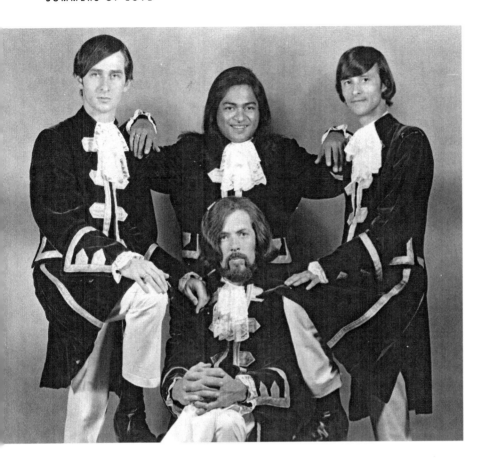

Doug described 1967 as his year of dropping out. He put together a band that
he continued to call the Sir Douglas Quintet, though the sets they played bore
little resemblance to the Tejano-flavored pop of "She's About a Mover." Doug
and whatever band he pulled together played at the Avalon some nights for
little more than tips in jars. He made his base of operations, but also his family home, in the hilltop tract house in Prunedale. Its occupants were Doug,
Violet, their numerous children, a poodle called Bourgeois, Violet's mother,
whom the kids called Nanny, and a rotation of Doug's guests who slept on a
sofa. Granny Sahm was also a frequent visitor. Some of the band's gigs during
those months were in the Los Angeles area. They were playing at the Whisky

Augie Meyers with promotional photo of his band Lord August
and the Visions of Lite. Augie and others declined at first to
move to San Francisco. Photo courtesy of Shawn Sahm.

a Go Go in Hollywood one night when Doug struck up a conversation with a drummer who would play a large role in his future. Originally from Fort Worth, George Rains had first known Doug at a San Antonio club called the Cellar, when Doug was affecting a suit and pinky ring in the style of T-Bone Walker. Rains now had a gig playing drums in a topless bar in a bowling alley near the L.A. airport. Doug asked if he would be interested in helping him put together a blues band. Rains quit his job and drove up Highway 101, where he found that while Prunedale had its charms, it was not exactly Monterey by the sea, as Doug had suggested. In a series of short, lively essays, Rains wrote that initially they spent their time smoking dope, dropping acid, and playing touch football with the kids. They feasted on Nanny's cooking and lay around listening to rhythm and blues and jazz. "Violet said it was like having two more kids hanging around the house. 'Just what I need!'"

Trailing after the three children from Violet's previous marriage, Doug's daughter Dawn was a four-year-old, and Shawn was two. Their brother Shandon would join the throng in 1969. One day out in the woods the kids got

Shandon Sahm with one of his favorite magazines at home in the Soap Creek Mansion. Photo courtesy of Shawn Sahm.

in some poison ivy. Their cheeks and lips turned a splotchy bright red and swelled up so badly that their attempts to speak were nothing but thick-tongued jabber. Just then Doug and George Rains wandered in sky-high on acid. Bad trip there, for a while.

Dawn recalled those days, "Dad was gone so much of the time, then he'd come back so skinny and gaunt he looked like a skeleton. Mom and my grandmother, who lived in a trailer on the back of the place, would fatten him up. He was really fond of Nanny's oatmeal." Shawn's childhood memories included one Christmas at the house in the Salinas Valley. "We woke up at dawn and were around the tree dying to tear into those presents. Pop said, 'Wait a minute, wait a minute, I've gotta get my groove, too!' And he came out with his pipe and big jar of pot." But the Christmases were also steeped in sentimentality and allegiance to down-home tradition. "He always got out his acoustic guitar," said Dawn, "and led us all in singing 'Rudolph the Red-Nosed Reindeer' and 'Frosty the Snowman.' One year there was an earthquake on Christmas morning—a small one, but it was strong enough that the tree started to topple over. I have this memory of Dad to the rescue—staggering around the living room with his arms around that tree."

Shawn recalled days when his dad would load them in the car and take them for rides that wound up at the house of Jerry Garcia. A lawyer named Brian Rohan, who represented the Grateful Dead, landed Doug a deal with Mercury Records and its sister labels Smash and Phillips. Doug soon had the band members driving sports cars and living in Marin County. The bandleader would roll in for rehearsals and gigs in his Cadillac. He talked a good game with club owners,

Shawn Sahm in New York for the Atlantic sessions. Photo courtesy of Shawn Sahm.

and they got more work than they could handle. They honed their material in Northern California bars where greased hair was the rule and the parking lots were a combat zone of brawls. The new sound was "seriously drug-induced R&B," said George Rains. "Psychedelic Wilson Pickett, Otis Redding on acid." Sometimes they were tight and driven, sometimes loose and floppy as laundry on a windblown line.

The only original member of the Sir Douglas Quintet who went into a San Francisco studio with Doug in the spring of 1968 was the sax player Frank Morin, and there were four new musicians in the booming horn section, including the gifted sax player and fellow connoisseur of pot, Martin Fierro. And, as it happened, Mercury had just contracted with Dan Healy to engineer the recordings of its San Francisco acts for one year. In those days San Francisco only had three recording studios—the crowd of them would come in the Seventies and Eighties. The Trident Records Studio was owned by the Kingston Trio, but the folk music vogue was almost finished, and the studios were for rent. Doug inherited in Dan Healy the wizard of mixing boards and amps who had gone a long way toward creating the myth of the Grateful Dead. The resulting album, *Sir Douglas Quintet + 2 = (Honkey Blues)*, was almost nothing like the San Antonio sound that had brought Doug so far. (On seeing the album title Fierro would remark that their leader had difficulty counting, since the band actually had nine members.) Augie Meyers's Vox was replaced by the jazz-oriented piano of Wayne Talbert, a new hire from Houston. There were plenty of bouquets tossed in the airs of the psychedelic period—lyrics about hippies grooving in ecstasy under the redwoods and cuts titled "Can You Dig My Vibrations" and "You Never Get Too Big and You Sure Don't Get Too Heavy, That You Don't Stop and Have to Pay Some Dues Sometime." But it was rhythm and blues and soul, and it was surprisingly tight, with few of the wandering, self-indulgent solos for which San Francisco bands like Moby Grape and Blue Cheer were famous. Doug's singing had never been stronger.

Many devotees of Doug's music contend that *Honkey Blues* is one of his most accomplished records. Certainly nobody else in San Francisco was then playing music quite like that. The cuts that hold up best are "Sell a Song" and "I'm Glad for Your Sake (But Sorry for Mine)." The former song was over five minutes long, and it ended with an extended jazz mix of piano and horns. It had the kind of blues narrative that Doug only wrote on occasion. A suitcase was packed; a kid was staring at his dad knowing that he wouldn't be making this house his home anymore; the dad was going off to San Francisco; and didn't the woman who'd treated him so badly believe he could still find some guy he could sell a song to? Didn't she think some girl would still think he was groovy?

Johnny Perez—also known in the circle as "J.P." or "Little Drummer Johnny"—was the former boxer who had gotten Doug out of jams and played with him before they formed the Quintet. After the Corpus Christi bust he moved out to L.A., where he was associated with a studio called Amigos de Musica. Doug nostalgically credited him as a sort of producer in absentia on *Honkey Blues*. Life in California was good, but Doug wished he could share the bounty with more of his pals from San Antonio's West Side. One of the best songs began with a trilling of Mexican acoustic guitar and a spoken tribute in Spanish to friends and bygone days in Texas; then Doug was saying mournfully, "It's been about two years since I left my home down in Texas. I miss a lot of my old friends down there. I'd like to send this song to y'all. It goes back to the old Blue Note and Tiffany days." As the band was bringing home the love lament of "I'm Glad for Your Sake (But Sorry for Mine)" the horns waned and Doug played a lively solo of precise country fiddle. The finale veered off into another piano jazz riff, then came a discordant squawk of saxophone, and Doug congratulated the players, "This gig's over, let's go home. That's too much."

In November 1968 *Rolling Stone* published its big story about the Texas presence in San Francisco music and the cover that featured Doug, Shawn, and their cowboy hats. The issue also contained the magazine's first review of a record by Doug. The reviewer lavished praise on *Honkey Blues* for its allegiance to rhythm and blues in the vein of Bobby "Blue" Bland and Horace Silver, and the lyrical "real jazz" of the horn arrangements. "As one conscientious critic, record-buyer, and music-digger to another, this one's really got it," the writer concluded. "It's got them groovy blues and that pretty gospel and that down home, country righteous good tone to it. The record makes me dance around and sing along."

The reviewer was Boz Scaggs, a musician of no small accomplishment and future in his own right.

Ralph J. Gleason, a veteran pop and jazz critic and cofounder of *Rolling Stone*, wrote imperiously in his *San Francisco Chronicle* review that he'd like to pull up the drawbridge and stop the traffic of outlander bands across the moat, except for one. "There is little originality aside from the original San Francisco bands. The only band I have heard play blues recently that was really listen-able in a musical sense (rather than volume and rhythm to be experienced in a physical sense) is Sir Douglas, and he is great just because he doesn't do it like the others."

The rock magazine *Circus* went even further: "*Honkey Blues* is most assur-edly a landmark in American music."

———

The Mercury contract also gave Doug a chance to start producing records. In one famous San Francisco session that did not bear fruit, the recording artist on hand was Chuck Berry. The brown-eyed handsome man and self-proclaimed father of rock and roll had abundant vices, but they did not include spending time with hippies who were doing drugs in a studio. Berry blew up at Doug and the session players Doug had, then stormed into the control room to find the Man, whoever he was, and protest further—and found that everyone in there was getting loaded, too. That was the end of the creative alliance of Doug Sahm and Chuck Berry.

But many musicians loved working with Doug, once they finally got started. Along with having gifts as a player and singer, he was a tremendous arranger, able to bring out the best of their collaborations mid-song, on the spot. Not that his personal faults didn't spill over into his craft. Some knew him as the king of the manic-depressives, and sidemen regularly complained that when it came time to pay them, that was when he started scamming. After all, he had learned his tricks on the business side from Huey Meaux.

And his personal life was unsettled, to put it mildly. In the wake of *Honkey Blues* Doug alienated his wife Violet and his friend Travis Rivers by running off with Rivers's wife for a while. In retaliation Rivers talked George Rains and the horn players Martin Fierro and Frank Morin into leaving Doug's band for Mother Earth, another group led by Texas exiles. Rivers found another tran-scendent singer, Tracy Nelson, and fell in love with her, just as he had when he ushered Janis Joplin to San Francisco. Rivers said he wept on hearing Nelson's audition, that he couldn't believe he'd been that lucky twice.

Sometime during this period Violet spoke her mind into a recorder in a slow drawl, as a small child babbled in agreeable reply. "What I'm gonna do is

I'm gonna find me a big old strong cowboy with big old strong arms that can hold me real tight. And I don't care if he's got a big old Lone Star beer gut or whatever it is you say—because that's what turns me on. Not these longhaired hippie rock and rollers . . . no guts about them at all, and they scream at their old ladies, and they're sweet to their chicks, well, that's *bullshit* with two T's!"

Despite the effusive praise the latest album won for Doug and his band in San Francisco, it did not sell well or command much attention elsewhere. Mercury executives sent word to Doug that though they liked *Honkey Blues,* business was business, and they had to show a profit. Doug later grumbled that it "would have been a hit outside San Francisco, too, but the band was just too freaky to tour. So they told us, 'Get back to that old groove.'"

Band of six, including Augie. Promotional photo arranged by Mercury Records. Photo courtesy of Shawn Sahm.

The Real Old Texas Me

Doug *was never one to brood over his setbacks* or dig in his heels, and with a veteran's practicality he knew that instead of taking fifteen people to a gig for three or four thousand dollars, he could take five and make the same money. He wasted little time trying to get back in his record company's good graces. Setting aside his hopes for the big blues band, he talked Johnny Perez into coming up from Hollywood to play the drums again and finally coaxed Augie into coming out from Texas. Another addition was the bass player Harvey Kagan, who had played with Augie in the Goldens. Once more, all the members of the Quintet were players Doug had known back in San Antonio.

They recorded *Mendocino* in San Francisco and Hollywood in September 1968. The album began with Doug's announcement: "The Sir Douglas Quintet is back, and I'd like to thank all the beautiful friends, and all the beautiful vibrations. We love you." Huey Meaux claimed that Doug had been living in Mendocino with a sixteen-year-old, and that when she left him for someone else and moved up to Oregon, it really set him back. In any case, without shame, a few weeks before his twenty-seventh birthday, he launched the title song with the line *"Teeny bopper, my teenage lover . . ."* The song revolved

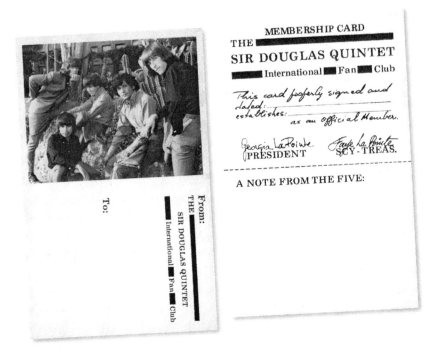

MEMBERSHIP CARD

THE ▬▬▬▬▬▬▬▬▬▬

SIR DOUGLAS QUINTET

▬▬▬▬ International ▬ Fan ▬ Club

This card properly signed and
dated:
establishes:
            as an official Member.

Georgia LaPointe   Faye La Pointe
PRESIDENT   SCY-TREAS.

A NOTE FROM THE FIVE:

To:

From:
THE
SIR DOUGLAS QUINTET
International ▬ Fan ▬ Club

around the image of two kids longing for a time when they walked in a park and made love beside a river. The lyrics were banal, but Augie was back in force, pumping away on the Vox. "Aw, play it, Augie!" Doug shouted on the take that made the record. The Quintet had pulled it off and hit pay dirt on the charts and radio playlists again. "Mendocino" reached number 27 on the U.S. singles charts, was a bigger hit in Europe, and Doug led the Quintet in a second appearance on the still weighty and prestigious *American Bandstand*. Engineered by Dan Healy, the *Mendocino* album showed that Doug and his friends could bring sustained brilliance from concept to the studio to record stores to playlists of the major FM radio stations. The horn duo of Frank Morin and Martin Fierro came together nicely, and as a complement to Augie's Vox, Doug showed off his stabbing three-finger style of playing the piano. And he stepped out front on this record and demonstrated what a fine guitar player he was. Playing a lead solo in a rousing remake of "She's About a Mover," he exulted in a droll aside about the hype of the local bands: "Where'd you get that freaky guitar player? Must have learned it out here!"

Photo of the original Sir Douglas Quintet and member card for the Sir Douglas Quintet International Fan Club. Provided courtesy of Shawn Sahm.

Mendocino did not wallow in awe of the terrain and fashion of California. To the contrary, the music revealed how homesick Doug was for Texas. The attitude stood out in his grieving cover of "If You Really Want Me to I'll Go" by Delbert McClinton, the young roadhouse veteran and harmonica stylist from Fort Worth, and in the comically disenchanted "Lawd, I'm Just a Country Boy in This Great Big Freaky City."

Doug's philosophy as an artist was contained in a single premise: finding and protecting his groove. How could he be expected to make music that put the audience in a groove, he reasoned, if he wasn't grooving himself? It was a self-centered and at times childish obsession. But despite its teenybop-pop title track, the album *Mendocino* was the work of a grown-up with a great deal of torment and regret in his psyche, and Doug delivered what was arguably the finest song he would ever write. This one posed a more detailed scene that began with a young man telling a lover that he was leaving her. "At the Crossroads" was a deeply personal and heartfelt piece; Doug knew the clock was running out on his ability to run wild and still maintain a marriage. Clichés of hippie-speak—such as being "wigged out"—were brushed aside by the poetry, power, and just plain good singing that climaxed with the chorus's closing lines: *"You just can't live in Texas / If you don't have a lot of soul."*

As *if an omen of good fortune,* a few days after the band emerged from the studio Doug received a congratulatory letter from his probation officer at the U.S. district court in Corpus Christi: his probation was terminated and his conviction set aside. But while all things might now be rosy in Texas, strife continued

Doug with cover of the band's LP *The Best of the Sir Douglas Quintet.* Photo courtesy of Shawn Sahm.

to build in Prunedale. "Mom was so sick of hippies," Shawn recalled, "sick of hairy people she didn't know sacked out on her couch and floor. She'd call him up at a girlfriend's house and let him have it. At home we'd hear her yelling, 'Douglas, we don't have any diapers!' He'd be out in the woods yelling back, '*Why can't you just groove?*'"

Mercury followed up the hit with single releases of "At the Crossroads" and "Dynamite Woman"—a jumpy sing-along that proved to be one of his most durable standards. The response to *Mendocino* and release and promotion of the singles sent the band on a triumphant tour of Europe, which postponed any resolution of the conflict at home.

They came back and appeared on Hugh Hefner's TV series, *Playboy after Dark*. Doug had a pal from San Antonio named Atwood Allen who was his favorite backup singer and also a very gifted songwriter. Atwood was large, un-kempt, and hairy—his favorite attire was a pair of overalls. The producers took one look at him and told Doug there was no way he was going to be on camera with Hefner and his crowd. "But we've gotta have him," said Doug, referring to the music. So a compromise was reached in which Atwood had a mike and sang his harmony while standing behind a curtain.

The conceit of the show was that it took place at an ordinary stand-around party in Hefner's mansion. Hefner turned away from a conversation with actor Michael Caine and, reaching over a tray of hors d'oeuvres, observed to Doug that the Quintet had made a Top 40 splash but then had fallen out of sight. Doug, who wore a cowboy hat and silk scarf, his sideburns now bushy and grown far down his jaws, explained smoothly that it took a while to make the transition from Texas to San Francisco. Hefner asked him about their experi-ence in England. "It was good, we want to go back," answered Doug. "They hadn't seen too many southern people at that time." Then Hefner invited them onstage, and they delivered "Mendocino" and "She's About a Mover" with aplomb, dancers no more than a yard from the small stage. Holding his pipe, Hefner showed off his moves with a gorgeous brunette in a dress cut to her navel. Doug couldn't help smiling and cutting his eyes at the players—this was *American Bandstand* for overprivileged adults.

When Shawn Sahm was old enough to wonder why his dad hadn't played at Woodstock, Doug said that nobody knew that one was going to be the mother of pop festivals, and that to get to the farm they were going to have to fly in storm-prone weather by helicopter, and he wouldn't risk that. He liked to note that two weeks before Woodstock, the Quintet *had* played the Atlantic City Pop Festival amid a lineup that included the Byrds, Canned Heat, Joe Cocker, Janis Joplin, Joni Mitchell, Creedence Clearwater Revival, Little Richard, Santana, and Frank Zappa.

On a roll, the Quintet hurried back into the studio. Huey Meaux, who had by now done his time, was allowed to come back as producer, and *Together after Five* came out in December 1969, just six months after *Mendocino*. Some critics trashed it. Doug shrugged off the poor reviews, saying he was unhappy with the record's production values. But even more than *Mendocino*, *Together after Five* dropped broad hints that the charms of California had grown stale for him. With *norteño* acoustic guitar, blasts of Mexican-style trumpets, and a verse sung in Spanish, "Nuevo Laredo" told a tale of an evening in the Boys' Town red-light district beside the Rio Grande; a gringo played the blues and the crowd sang along until the fun ended with the inevitable squabble over a raven-haired girl that sent the gringo running for the safety of Texas soil. "Dallas Alice" was the story of a roughneck in love with a rich man's daughter, but Doug let the story trail off and grew enamored with the variations a jazz singer could bring to rhyming the names of the city and girl. Uproarious, almost giggling, he revived the Leadbelly shoot-out song "Son of Bill Baety," making it into a dreamlike medley that changed the scene from a black juke joint with a man shot dead on the floor to happy doggerel about cowboys: "*come a cow pie yippie yippie yea.*" His singing on several cuts borrowed from Bob Dylan's style of accenting the close of a verse. On one cut titled "I Don't Want to Go Home," Doug again showed remorse over his inability to choose between his irresponsibility and his marriage vows. "*I got too free,*" he sang, "*and forgot I had a family.*"

—

The next album, 1 + 1 + 1 = 4, was largely drawn from outtakes of the *Honkey Blues* and *Mendocino* sessions. Doug was always playing games with the record company and the credits, trying to do favors to musicians who might have dropped by the studio but never picked up an instrument. On this record the prankster went further, citing as songwriters on two cuts "T. Murray"—his mother-in-law, whom the kids called Nanny—and "V. Morris," his dear wife Violet. Camouflaged in the welter of names on the liner notes were a core band

Mercury promotional photos of Augie Meyers (*above*) and Doug (*right*)
during "Mendocino" period. Photos courtesy of Shawn Sahm.

that now had Augie on keyboards, Harvey Kagan on bass, and (back from Mother Earth) Frank Morin on sax and George Rains on drums. But Doug recorded the most talked-about cut, "Be Real," in a Nashville studio with a producer named Jerry Kennedy and a band of session players. With vocals credited to Doug Sahm and Wayne Douglas—a transposition of his birth names that had become his country-western alter ego—Doug and Kennedy made a serious attempt to carve a niche for him in the country music of Nashville. "Be Real" received some airplay, and he returned to Nashville on occasion, recording another version of "I Don't Want to Go Home" and the lovelorn "I Wanna Be Your Mama Again." But his voice was new to the audience he wanted to reach, and despite his bona fides, Doug was a hard sell in Nashville. He could never convince the gatekeepers there that he wasn't a hippie trying to run a scam.

Violet, who was usually left out of his music business, which was fine with her, heard a cassette tape brought into her house by her kids, who had gotten to be friends with the bass player of a Chicano garage band. They came from families of factory and farm workers. She kept the tape of the youths' garage band and finally got Doug to listen to it. He called the youths to the house, announced that he was going to get them a record deal, and when they next saw him he said the deal was done with Columbia's Epic label. Oh, Doug added, in the meeting he and the record executives had decided the band had a new name—they were now Louie and the Lovers.

Handsome and good-natured, Louie Ortega was the band's lead guitarist and singer and songwriter. Ortega grew up listening mostly to country-western and Hispanic music in his home, but his enthusiasm soon leaped to the Beatles, Motown soul groups, and Creedence Clearwater Revival. Producing the record, Doug took them into a San Francisco studio and pushed the kids to do it all in eighteen hours. He wrote in his blurb, "Louie's songwriting is tuned into today. It's real Chicano, man." The record did contain lively Farfisa organ play and one tune about driving to Brownsville to hear some South Texas rock and roll. But Doug's records had more Chicano inflection than *Rise* by Louie and the Lovers. It was California music, flowing electric guitars and breezy harmonies—much the same style as the Eagles, but the kids' singing was at times superior, and there was a genuineness of connection to the stories in the songs that Louie wrote. Ed Ward, a pop music critic who had been noticed and turned loose by Jann Wenner, gave the record a rave review in *Rolling Stone.*

Could the music business really be so easy? Of course not, but what did these seventeen-year-olds know? With Doug's help they maneuvered out of the contract with Epic into one with Atlantic. Their career guardians were now the legendary producers Jerry Wexler and Tom Dowd. Soon they were on their way to studios where Dowd had engineered *Layla and Other Assorted Love Songs* by Eric Clapton and his wild band of Americans, Derek and the Dominos. "That was something," Ortega told Ward, laughing. "We were just out of high school, and I remember our drummer had never been in a plane, and Atlantic sent the company Lear Jet for us and flew us down to Criteria Studios in Miami." Wexler produced the second album, but it went unreleased, and a fire later destroyed the master tape. The drummer got married, and the teen band fell apart. But they influenced bands like Los Lonely Boys, Ortega would play in Doug's bands for years to come, and from a base in San Luis Obispo he recorded highly praised solo albums. "And for years," he said, "Doug was always calling me back and working me into his bands. He was kind of my musical father."

Violet Sahm with her mother in Texas.
Photo courtesy of Shawn Sahm.

Those months saw him going through material and projects like a buzz saw. He produced three singles by the Tribe Records swamp pop rocker Roy Head and one by a rhythm-and-blues hero from the Eastwood Country Club days, Junior Parker. The Quintet put out an EP on which they sang "Mendocino," "Nuevo Laredo," and two songs in Spanish. In a burst of political incorrectness, the ever-loyal *Rolling Stone* declared him Chicano of the Year.

In January 1971 Doug headed home with *The Return of Doug Saldaña*. The title referred to the honorary name his friends on the West Side had given him as a teenager. After an absence of five years, he drove to San Antonio, where he picked up Rocky Morales, the tenor sax player; Jack Barber, the bass player and part-time barber; Leonidas Baety, a maracas shaker who had played with Doug in the early days and baked doughnuts for a living; and Atwood Allen, the talented backup vocalist and songwriter. Augie Meyers and Johnny Perez also joined the band, and they journeyed to record with Huey Meaux in Houston, where it had all begun six years earlier. They were all one big happy family, except for one minor detail, at least as Augie told the story.

Augie claimed that he and Doug were talking in California one day and he told his old friend that he had an idea for a cover photograph that he wanted to put on a solo record. Augie would be sitting on his front porch in Bulverde holding a Big Red soda. (Big Red is a regionally distributed soft drink that's dosed with caffeine and tastes like cough syrup, without the thickness. It's an acquired taste and a Texas thing—a hip relic.) When *The Return of Doug Saldaña* came out, it showed Doug at his ease in a rocking chair with his legs crossed and his expression pensive. Looking fit and eager, he wore jeans, boots, a plaid cowboy shirt, and a dark cowboy hat, his hair long in back but with his sideburns trimmed. He held a bottle of Big Red and was sitting on Augie's front porch in Bulverde, Texas. Augie claimed Doug had gone out to his property and staged the picture while Augie was still in California. "Look at the photograph," Augie said. "The screen door's padlocked. My fishing pole's standing in a corner. He used my house: it was my idea. When I got after him he said, 'Aw, well, I didn't know when you'd get around to it, how soon your record would come out.' Good friends, yeah. Sometimes I wondered. He owed me some enchiladas for that one."

The album contained stirring saxophone solos from Rocky Morales, Doug shouting a blues tribute to T-Bone Walker in a favorite song, "Papa Ain't Salty,"

and he again affected the vocal delivery of Bob Dylan in "Stoned Faces Don't Lie." He anguished over drought in "Oh Lord, Please Let It Rain in Texas," and he played a nice jazz piano solo in "The Gypsy." But the autobiographical cast of his songwriting and brooding state of mind came across strongly in "Me and My Destiny" and "Texas Me." "*I wonder what happened to that man inside the real old Texas me.*"

He made it clear that it was time for major changes in his life, but he was still chasing that elusive rainbow, enduring fame. He offered a glimpse of how his mind perceived the margin between stardom and oblivion in the album's high point—his cover of the 1959 blues hit "Wasted Days and Wasted Nights," which he began with the introduction: "This is a song written by the great Freddy Fender. Freddy, this is for you, wherever you are." One year you could be a star with young girls fainting at the sound of your voice; and the next you could be forgotten and hoeing weeds between cotton rows on a prison in Louisiana.

"The move back to Texas," said Shawn, "was really about Mom wanting out of this marriage, out of California. Dawn and I were in an uproar; we didn't want to go. Pop was saying, 'Hey, it's cool, we're gonna groove, you'll love it there.'" Amid all this conflict, in July 1971 *Rolling Stone* put Doug on its cover for the second time. This time he posed bareheaded, with his hands clasped in front of his chin, smiling like he had the world all figured out. "Sir Douglas Goes Home," the cover announced.

Doug and Augie, bringing the San Antonio sound to Austin. Photo copyright © Brian Maurer.

Doug captivated many writers and counted a number of them as friends, but none described the world he came from as vividly as Chet Flippo in *Rolling Stone*. Chet and his wife became good friends of Doug and Violet. In the profile, Violet seemed cheerful enough, and Doug's mother brought out an old picture of him seated at the Cabaret Club in Bandera behind his steel guitar with some Pearl beer bottles underfoot. She reminisced that instead of passing the kitty, the patrons threw quarters and half dollars at him. Bootie was out there scooping up the take; she said he got ninety-two dollars that night. Doug pulled another photo out of the album and seemed almost joyous in his nostalgia. It was an Uncle Bill who had been a fearsome, gun-carrying bouncer in the wild bars of San Antonio.

Doug later took Flippo for a spin around old haunts on the West Side, and parts of his rhapsody bear repeating: "Man, I've played some places that were turned out *twice* a night. Bullets'd start flyin' and you'd just have to hit the deck. I've seen cats shot off the bandstand. Oh, hell *yes*. San Antone's a gunslingin' town, it's a *fact*. . . . The West Side. Man, there's places down here where the cops won't come. Dig—cats sittin' on the corner with no clothes on, shootin' smack. . . . Cats with machine guns in their cars. Shoo. *Beautiful*."

What a curious set of things to be ecstatic about! But this was material for his earthy songs, not a morality play. And he was home again. The man was on a tear.

Ed Ward, who later was a co-author of Rock of Ages: Rolling Stone's History of Rock and Roll, wrote about Doug throughout his career. They had a complicated and at times rocky relationship. Ward was always suggesting that Doug's records never quite measured up to his talent or the writer's critical standards. He reviewed *Mendocino* and its title track: "The lyrics are printed there on the back of the album. Please don't look at them. They're not very good. But if you hear the song twice, you'll be humming it and it'll make you feel good." In payback Doug once conned Ward into believing that, even with a name like Sahm, he came from a family that was Lebanese. The writer dutifully committed the lie to print, and it would follow Doug beyond the pale. But Ward wrote about him tirelessly, and in sleeve notes for a retrospective of the Mercury years, *Sir Doug's Recording Trip,* he offered a gem of insight into the artist's state of mind.

Before Doug left California, a director named Bill Gordon offered him a role

in a movie called *Cisco Pike*. The movie starred Kris Kristofferson as an ex-convict musician and drug dealer, Gene Hackman as a crooked cop, Karen Black as a spacey sexpot, and the supporting cast included Harry Dean Stanton and an Andy Warhol protégée called Viva! (her exclamation point). Doug was essentially hired to play himself. Doug and his band contributed one of the great cannabis-loving songs, "Michoacán," to the score, but Doug informed Ward that this lucky break was all about music on the radio, not the movie.

Doug enthused, "This is a hit, man!" Ward replied that a song about the primo dope of the day would never get played on the radio. Doug answered with eyes aglow: "But only the heads really know that: over at the record company they think this song's about a state in Mexico!"

As Ward predicted, disk jockeys were wary of playing the song, and they also failed to discover the flip side, the gorgeous six-minute-long "Westside

Doug cheerfully mocking a photographer in a recording session. Photo courtesy of Shawn Sahm.

Blues Again." Doug was disappointed once more in his quest for the monster hit. Still, he turned in what may be the funniest thirty-eight-second acting debut ever filmed.

In the scene Kristofferson, who was in his heyday as a glamorous hunk, tried to hand off a demo tape to a gaunt record producer with glasses and limp shoulder-length hair. Wearing jeans, boots, and a yellow western shirt, Doug greeted Kristofferson with a burst of air guitar, near-yodeling scat, and phony nostalgia for their days playing together. "Get it *on,* man!"

The ex-con nodded tolerantly, then wondered in a growl if the producer was ever tempted to "get out of that border bag and try something different."

Doug started squirming like he feared a mama scorpion with a cargo of babies might be crawling up his back. "I don't know, man, you know me, man, I'm a simple cat, I dig simple stuff, man: you know where the groove is at, that California thing don't get it," he squealed, "that far-out-in-space business—play the *real* thing!" He was waving his arms and talking so fast he got tongue-tied. He almost guffawed but instead seemed to appreciate the warble of gib-berish rolling off his tongue for what it was. To his credit, the director would decide that this take was the one to keep. Doug shrugged. "You know, man."

Kristofferson wagged his head and continued gamely with the scene. "Aw, yeah. I guess that's what makes horse racing, ain't it?"

"I guess what you can do, man," said Doug, handing back the tape, in a hurry to get rid of him now, "when Jesse gets here, he'll know what to do, man, you cats will get it together, it'll come together, you know where the groove is, just work it out now . . . I love you."

With a slap on the old bud's shoulder, the music man was gone.

Crossroads

Things did not work out in Texas quite the way Doug hoped. Doug was always one to drop in on people, and on the long trek from Salinas County to San Antonio he took advantage of the hospitality of some kinfolks who lived in West Texas. His stepson Ron was taking a bath when he saw a condom. Not knowing what it was, he blew it up, tied it off, and came out batting it in the air like a balloon. The kinfolks, who were devout Christians, exploded in a fury and kicked them all out in the middle of the night.

While the big *Rolling Stone* profile made its splash and *The Return of Doug Saldaña* circulated among disk jockeys and buyers for record stores, for several weeks the rock star and his brood wound up living out at Bulverde with Augie and his family. "I put him to work helping chop wood," Augie said. "It was cold that winter, and all the heat we had was a potbellied stove." When Doug found a place for them to live he and Violet fell into a cycle of battling and fitfully reconciling—the dance of longtime lovers on the verge of calling it quits. Violet's children from her previous marriage were growing into their teens, and they eventually drifted out of close touch with the stepfather who'd spent eight years supporting and helping raise them. But Dawn was eight, Shawn was six, and Shandon was two when the family arrived back in Texas. Doug didn't want to lose them, though he was in clear danger of losing their mother.

Dawn enjoyed the warm and cuddly relationship known by many firstborn daughters—she was always her daddy's baby girl. "First thing, he took us to Brackenridge Park to ride the train that winds through there," she said, "and when it got to a tunnel he started talking in this scary voice and told us about the time some men jumped out of the dark and robbed this little choo-choo ridden by parents and their kids." San Antonio was rich with memories of Doug's own childhood, but it also confronted him with stark new realities. Violet went to work as a legal secretary and was promptly courted by her boss's brother, a young man named Dee Huffman. Shawn recalled: "We moved in this house in Balcones Heights, and Dee, who had a heart of gold and would become our stepfather, entered the picture. Mom had six kids by the time she was twenty-six; she was a beautiful lady, understand, but she did have some baggage. Dee was this guy in his mid-twenties who was willing to take all that on. He came into our lives and began to use words like *restrictions*. We're going to have some *discipline*. We're going to do some *chores*. We'd never heard that language in our lives."

Their idea of being reprimanded in California was when they'd get into their dad's stash. He'd run after them, hunched over like a monkey, yelling, "Gimme back my pipe!" They'd jump in their beds and pull the covers up over their heads, in hysterics. "Well, our life was changing," said Shawn, "and so was Pop's. He was hanging in there. I remember one Thanksgiving when Dee did the cooking. And there was Dad, turning on all the charm, carving the turkey. Dad didn't really get it, even after the divorce. He kind of liked it that way."

In San Antonio Doug treasured friends like the West Side sax player Rocky Morales, the old western-swing fiddler J. R. Chatwell, and the outsized harmonist Atwood Allen. He had so much personal history invested in the city and its music, but even as he lingered there he was moving on. Except for the picture of him taken in Hank Williams's lap and the odd gig with the original Quintet, Doug had little experience in Austin. But in California he had known and jammed with many players who testified to its magnet of creativity. Austin was half the size of San Antonio and did not possess as rich a mix of ethnic history and intercourse, but the University of Texas and the jobs, news coverage, and wild parties associated with the state legislature were alluring to writers, painters, photographers, musicians, and moviemakers who had grown up in Texas's

much more conservative towns and cities. Though the people in power at the state capitol were reactionaries in their politics more often than not, Austin had long been the raunchiest and most bohemian town in Texas.

At the start of the Sixties, musicians who wanted to get paid for playing rock and roll covered hits of the day at dances of fraternities and sororities. But that meant they were working, learning. During that time a folk music and proto-hippie community emerged that was affiliated with faculty and students at the university. A noted center of ferment and hell-raising was a once-distinguished residence that had been carved into a bohemian tenement called the Ghetto. Suspicious that it nested a bunch of godless, dope-taking communists, the Austin police compiled a secret intelligence report that, when revealed by freedom of information laws, included a prose stylist, Billy Lee Brammer, who had written a highly praised novel of politics, *The Gay Place,* and a singer of alleged low morals named Janis Joplin. She played an Autoharp in those days and was remembered for her version of "Silver Threads and Golden Needles." Some fraternity members took a strong disliking to her and cruelly succeeded

Doug with his San Antonio pal, the noted western swing fiddler J. R. Chatwell. Photo courtesy of Shandon Sahm.

in getting her elected the ugliest man on campus. The folksingers performed in a Methodist youth center near the campus and a gas station that had been turned into a convivial beer joint by a Jimmy Rodgers–style yodeler, Kenneth Threadgill, who became a father figure for Joplin. Another player was a graduate student named Bill Malone, who wrote the authoritative history *Country Music, U.S.A.*

Later in the Sixties, small cafés on the black east side welcomed a few bands of white youths. The IL Club, said a young guitarist and songwriter named Bob Brown, "was the kind of place where older black people gathered in the afternoons to play dominoes. But here a bunch of cracker hippies marches down and starts playing so loud that food is flying off forks all over the neighborhood." Brown shared lead guitar duties in a popular band called the Conqueroo with Charlie Pritchard, the San Antonio native who had gone along for the fun in Corpus Christi of the Sir Douglas Quintet's end-of-the-year gig in 1965, and came home with his prized '36 Ford confiscated and with a felony drug charge on his record.

Following the lead of developments in California, a number of clubs had popped up in central and south Austin with names like the Old New Orleans, the Jade Room, Mother Earth, and the Continental Club. The Vulcan Gas Company, the biggest and most storied venue, opened on Congress Avenue, the main downtown street, and it played an important role in the development of Texas rock and roll. The Vulcan had dazzling light shows and gifted artists illustrating the posters, but its owners were continually strapped for revenue. All the money they made had to come off the gate, for they couldn't afford the state's licenses to sell beer or wine. The hippies in charge brought in storied black blues players like Mance Lipscomb and Lightnin' Hopkins and set an Austin stage for the talents of Steve Miller, Boz Scaggs, and Johnny Winter, who moved on to San Francisco and New York to sign recording contracts and win their fame.

The 13th Floor Elevators, the Conqueroo, and Shiva's Headband were Austin's leading rock-and-roll bands. The Elevators' guitarist and singer, Roky Erickson, had astounded Doug with his shrill vocals and garage-band guitar during the band's brief sojourn in San Francisco in late 1966. Erickson started using both his songwriting and his exposure at gigs to reflect on the possible holiness of his role in the universe. Years later the journalist Michael Hall described Erickson's torment and decline in a *Texas Monthly* retrospective: "At a November 1967 concert in Houston, he was afraid to walk onstage because he didn't want the crowd to see the eye in the middle of his forehead." By then the band's singular live show had degenerated into feedback- and drug-laden jams. When Bill Bentley, who was a devoted fan and booster of the Elevators, saw them in 1968, Roky stood with his back to the audience, singing a different song from what his bandmates were playing. "It was heartbreaking," Bentley told Hall. "I thought, 'It's over. How did *that* happen?'"

In early 1969 Erickson got busted for marijuana possession in Austin and was sent to a state hospital, where doctors diagnosed him as a schizophrenic and put him on an antipsychotic drug, Haldol. He walked out of the hospital without being discharged and was arrested again three months later. Facing a sentence of two years to life, he pleaded innocent by reason of insanity. A psychiatrist and the judge agreed with his argument. Though the judge declared him innocent, without delay he sent Erickson to the state's prison for the criminally insane in an East Texas town called Rusk, where he received multiple electric shock treatments and massive doses of Thorazine. For six years. He wrote a book of poems and rock lyrics called *Openers* that friends on the outside arranged to publish. One poem was called "Ye Are Not Crazy, Man."

Shiva's Headband also had a cult following in Texas and regular gigs at the Vulcan Gas Company, but couldn't withstand the number of times its leader and psychedelic fiddler, Spencer Perskin, was hauled to jail and court on marijuana busts. The Conqueroo made the pilgrimage to San Francisco, but they got some bad breaks that come with the territory of being musicians. A writer for *Rolling Stone* came out to talk to them and, picking up on something a Conqueroo member volunteered, instead wrote about the albino blues singer Johnny Winter, a nugget of publicity that led to his recording contract and six-figure advance. The Conqueroo realized they had arrived too late. "The scene was really starting to degenerate," said the guitarist and singer Bob Brown. "Haight Street smelled like piss, and a lot of little stores were closing down. All the people we thought were running around with flowers in their hair were now lying around with needles stuck in their necks."

When Doug moved back to Texas in 1971 and, fading the heat in his marriage, began to investigate Austin, the Elevators, the Conqueroo, and the Vulcan Gas

Company were history. (Broke and exhausted, the downtown club's owners had closed it a few months earlier.) But the music boom in Austin of the Sixties fueled a much greater explosion to come.

The growth of Austin as a significant American music town was directly related to the opening in 1970 of a big club called Armadillo World Headquarters. The building had begun as a sports arena that failed to live up to the hopes of its investors and builders. Elvis played there in 1955 when his hair was blond, peroxide or otherwise. The building was used as a National Guard armory for

some years, and then sat vacant. Spencer Perskin contributed Shiva's Headband's first royalty check to help get the place open, and the band played the first night of its operation. A young beer distributor named Eddie Wilson, an entertainment lawyer named Mike Tolleson, and an artist named Jim Franklin rented the hangarlike building in south Austin and gave the new club its evocative name. Franklin's graphics and murals of armadillos made the waddling critter a Texas icon. Franklin and another talented poster artist, Micael Priest, took turns introducing the bands with grandiose acts of their own and surreal costumes. Hank Alrich managed daily operations for most of the club's existence, and many people, including Wilson's then-wife Genie, worked to keep the enterprise running on a fairly even keel for nearly a decade, even though they never had an enforceable lease. With a beer and wine license, a big stage, a sophisticated sound system, and a commune of Houston exiles who captured a large archive of performances on well-shot video, they gave Austin a music venue in the league of the famed San Francisco and New York halls.

Important small clubs also gained footing—Castle Creek, the Saxon Pub, and the Continental Club—and some of the best venues weren't even clubs. Willie Nelson played to a genial mob scene in the showroom and service area of a friend and Ford dealer named Bill McMorris. My first awareness that something unique to Austin was afoot came in the spring of 1972 at a place called Hill on the Moon. In the hills west of town, it was nothing more than a cleared slope among juniper brakes with a stage and decent sound system. A poetry reading was followed that night by an electrifying set by a songwriter

Doug's return to Texas, concert at Armadillo World Headquarters, August 4, 1971. Photograph copyright © Burton Wilson, 1997.

named Michael Murphey who had a striking first album called *Geronimo's Cadillac*, a fast-growing range of songs, and an ace group of backup players who left their mark on Austin's music of the Seventies as the Lost Gonzo Band.

Suddenly Austin swarmed with singer-songwriters who looked like bearded hippies but wore cowboy hats and recruited fiddle and steel guitar players for their bands. The sound they brought to life was not entirely original—the Byrds had moved fondly if somewhat slickly through a country-rock phase in *Sweetheart of the Rodeo*. Jerry Garcia, who had first won recognition in San Francisco folk clubs as a banjo player, taught himself the pedal steel so he could play with the New Riders of the Purple Sage, before joining the Grateful Dead. Gram Parsons and Chris Hillman started the Flying Burrito Brothers, and Parsons then teamed up with Emmylou Harris, who was emerging as a standout country singer. The Band demonstrated the bittersweet grace of country in songs like "Up on Cripple Creek" and "The Night They Drove Old Dixie Down." (One of the pals Doug Sahm made in his peregrinations with Bob Dylan's crowd was Rick Danko, the charismatic bass player and tenor singer of the Band.) And on many songs, if not entire albums, Doug had refuted the notion that persons of any single political ideology and affiliation could monopolize country-western.

But in a stellar way the sound of Austin was bringing fun back to country and taunting hokey old Nashville. The originality of Austin country-rock lay in its layered echoes of gospel, blues of mostly rural vein, fiddle and steel players who had been schooled by listening to western swing, and Scotch-Irish folk standards that were now called bluegrass. And it conveyed a strong generational sense that did not capitulate to the ways of Dallas, Houston, and smaller hidebound cities but rather sifted through the better legacies and possibilities of Texas and found places—Austin, San Antonio, an oval of Hill Country towns and ranch country connecting the two cities—where living was tolerable, even enviable.

Driving it were artists who were far enough along in their careers to win recording contracts, though they relied on live gigs to make a living. Michael Murphey was a fussy and studious Dallas native who in Los Angeles had been a factory songwriter and reportedly had come close to landing a role in the faux-Beatles TV sitcom *The Monkees;* on his second record he coined a term that he grew to despise with a song called "Cosmic Cowboy Souvenir." Jerry

Jeff Walker, whose real name was Ronald Clyde Crosby, was an itinerant folk-singer from New York known for one 1968 hit, "Mr. Bojangles," which he'd written after a night in a New Orleans drunk tank. He liked to say he did not steal, but rather inherited, the Lost Gonzo Band from Murphey, but in any case they switched leaders en masse and gave Walker the rowdiest show in town. When another important figure, Steven Fromholz, composed his classic song-poem of small town life, "Texas Trilogy," he was a U.S. Navy electrician stationed in San Francisco; he left base on Thursday night liberty to perform in a little bar on Union Street. The enigmatic Willis Alan Ramsey wrote and sang one almost flawless album on Leon Russell's Shelter label, backed up by

Doug partaking a favorite pastime during the California years. Photo courtesy of Shawn Sahm.

friends of Russell who were among the country's finest session players; then he receded as far away as Ireland, trying to stop hearing the question of when he would finish the second record. He never did. Kinky Friedman, the son of a psychology professor in Austin and a former Peace Corpsman in Borneo, wielded country songwriting as a satirical weapon; he would later make his living as a novelist and run for governor, a quixotic venture that did not end well.

Musically aligned with Austin was the dusty and windblown city of Lubbock, which contributed its own distinctive sound and ambitious performers, and sent them on to Austin in an unbroken stream. The debts owed to Buddy Holly by singers, writers, and guitar players like Joe Ely, Jimmie Dale Gilmore, Butch Hancock, Gary P. Nunn, Jesse Taylor, and John Reed were more than echoes of style. Holly's dad actively encouraged them and helped some of them make their first records. Delbert McClinton spent his early boyhood years in Lubbock, but his parents moved to Fort Worth and he epitomized the honky-tonk nature of that unpretentious town—black blues joints along the Trinity River levees and volatile cowboy dives on the Mansfield and Jacksboro highways. McClinton was twenty-two when he added a sensual harmonica part on a song by Bruce Channel, "Hey Baby," that reached number 1 on the British charts. McClinton taught John Lennon to play the harmonica.

Willie Nelson was older than those performers. In his music, if not in actual age, he came out of a prior generation. Though Willie had not charted a Nashville hit in several years, he had a crowd of hard-core fans who followed him from beer joint to beer joint in small towns near Austin and San Antonio. About the time Doug Sahm left Prunedale, California, Willie moved from Ridgetop, Tennessee, to Houston for a short time, and then Austin. Hardly rolling in dough in those days, he rented an apartment for his family and himself in south Austin. Bill Bentley was then playing drums in a band called Lea Ann and the Bizarros. Bentley said, "We played a George McGovern for President benefit in the summer of '72 at Austin's Zilker Park. . . . There were probably four thousand people in the audience, most of them hippies, and most didn't know who he was. He had on a black cowboy hat, and he played his first song, and it was like, 'Whoa, who's that?' His charisma was so instantaneous. Those longhairs in the audience were completely pulled in. My feeling then was that's when he saw that hippies dug him. It was ground zero of redneck rock."

Others point to an April night in 1973 when Willie Nelson and his band played Armadillo World Headquarters for the first time. The Armadillo leaders and staff were uncertain how the concert would go. With clouds of marijuana smoke always pungent in the place—the Austin police chose to let that civil disobedience go—hippies mingled with Willie's redneck fans. But any hostility between the two audiences evaporated as they were swept up in the spell of Willie's jazz-inflected singing and his playing of a battered Martin's guitar in a style he called Spanish. He hired an exuberant band that rolled through a medley of his songs that sometimes in concerts filled up an entire set. Willie knew by then what he liked to smoke to take the edge off of things, and he was perhaps the first country musician of his time to grow a beard and long hair, but his revolt was really against the contracts, arrangements, and session bands that had been forced on him, even if he was a member of the Grand Ole Opry.

Nursing similar grudges was his friend Waylon Jennings, who had briefly been a member of Buddy Holly's Crickets, had won a 1968 country Grammy with an improbable cover of "MacArthur Park," that odd song about a cake left out in the rain, and was now living in Arizona. On the night he arrived with his band at the Armadillo World Headquarters, he was reported to have taken one look at the crowd and said, "What the shit have you got me into, Willie?" Billy Joe Shaver, Guy Clark, and other Texas-born singers followed Willie and Waylon into the rotation in Austin, if not continual habitation.

When Willie Nelson arrived in Austin, he was a legendary country-western songwriter who had cut his ties with Nashville. He had pulled out when his house burned down in the Tennessee countryside. He needed gigs and an expanded audience to keep paying the bills, and the following he developed in Austin had come of age respectful of Hank Williams and his contemporaries, but as teens they were more attuned to rock and roll—Elvis and Buddy Holly and Bob Dylan, the Beatles and Rolling Stones. Though Willie commanded the attention of younger musicians in Austin and was a generous spirit, most of them were more awed by the presence in town of Doug Sahm. He personified what those musicians wanted to be. He had twice been on the cover of *Rolling Stone*.

But Doug was in no position or state of mind to take the lead of some *movement.* For several months after heading back to Texas he had no permanent address. He chose to construct his life that way. The exact date when he moved

to Austin is difficult to establish, because he was in and out of town so much. Doug and Violet continued to battle and try to regain love's magic in San Antonio, then he'd take off on one of his patented jaunts, short or long, and then he would reappear and reassume the role of being Pop with the kids and trying to hold the family together.

Dawn was born July 4, 1963, and now the little girl coming into her teens resented the intrusion and required attendance at Willie Nelson's hot, dusty, chaotic Fourth of July Picnics. "I don't *wanta* go to Willie's Picnic on my birthday," she pleaded with her dad, who was always on the Picnic's bill. The Sahm children made the acquaintance of Austin in the backseat of their dad's Cadillac and the apartments of his girlfriends. Shawn recalled, "I know we blew it for him all the time. We'd go up to Austin to see him and a girlfriend would jump in the car saying, 'Hi, kids, sweeties!' And we couldn't remember which one she was and we'd call her by the wrong name." In fact they would do that to him on purpose. They would spout something they knew was sure to get him in trouble, then run outside giggling at his exasperated order: "Go get in the car!"

Doug, at far left, with his young admirer and protégé, Stevie Ray Vaughan. The woman seated to Vaughan's left is Doug's former flame, fondly known to his children as Pammy the K. Photograph by Darrell Shifflett.

Doug had some relationships that were more important and lasting than others. One of the more durable liaisons was with a woman they called Pammy the K. Doug met her at Soap Creek Saloon, where her friends included Stevie Ray Vaughan, who was then an émigré from Dallas accustomed to playing for a few dozen people. Shawn remembered one time when his dad's habits definitely got on the nerves of Pammy the K. "Pop was an old school guy. This was a man who had never in his life had to do his own laundry. He'd been staying with her a lot and, you know, running up her phone bill and things like that. One night she was doing the dishes, she suggested to him, 'Hey, why don't you help out, too?' They had a pretty good little spat, and I remember he flung open the cabinet and got this cup and a dishcloth, and he was really going after it with his index finger. 'Is this how you do it? Huh? Tell me! Is this how you do it?'"

Austin after Dark

xecutives, producers, and talent scouts of most record companies were skeptical that much of commercial value would come out of Austin, but Jerry Wexler of Atlantic Records had a hunch they were wrong. Wexler had grown up in the Bronx, Harlem, and Brooklyn playing stickball, hanging out in a pool hall, swimming in the Hudson River. He was drafted into the army in World War II but did not see combat; after his discharge, he finished work on a journalism degree in Kansas, which led to a staff job at *Billboard*. Wexler was the one who saw the future and changed the crude name of one of their charts, Race, to an evocative name that he coined, Rhythm and Blues. In 1952 Ahmet and Nesuhi Ertegun, the founders of Atlantic, brought Wexler in as a company partner. Atlantic made its early name and stake in the business by recording great jazz musicians, but Wexler and Tom Dowd, the nuclear physicist turned vanguard recording engineer and then producer, led Atlantic's move to broaden its base and position in the market.

During Wexler's first two years at Atlantic, the label had thirty songs in the Rhythm and Blues Top 10. By the time Wexler took an interest in Austin music, he had produced or coproduced hit records by LaVern Baker, Joe Turner, Clyde McPhatter, Ray Charles, Ivory Joe Hunter, Wilson Pickett, Etta James, Roberta

Doug in his prime onstage.
Photo courtesy of Shawn Sahm.

Flack, Aretha Franklin, and Otis Redding. Atlantic added a new country division that Wexler directed, and to appease the partners in New York the new venture was headquartered in Nashville. But after illuminating stops in Memphis and Muscle Shoals, Alabama, Wexler was not shy about letting it be known that he was looking for acts rooted as much in rhythm and blues as country-western. In defiance of the New York partners, he and Dowd effectively made Miami and Criteria Studios the home of Atlantic South. (Criteria was best known for the wild 1970 *Layla* sessions of Derek and the Dominos, who enlisted Duane Allman to complement Eric Clapton's guitar play following an all-night jam with the Allman Brothers. Allman was a Wexler pal and one of his favorite musicians.)

In his mid-sixties, Wexler was a producer of awe-inspiring reputation. According to a fascinating interview and career retrospective of Wexler by the *Austin Chronicle*'s Raoul Hernandez, his interest in Doug Sahm began when an Atlantic promo scout named Dickie Klein passed on tips that signing him would be a coup, and the veteran producer became a fan of the Quintet's Mercury albums. Doug claimed that they'd gotten to know each other when he was helping Louie and the Lovers get out of their contract with Epic and sign with Atlantic to record their ill-fated second album at Criteria. In any case, the timing was right for Wexler to make his overture. Doug was frustrated and resentful that neither *The Return of Doug Saldaña* nor any of the other Mercury releases had broken out after the success of *Mendocino*. Though Mercury sent the Quintet on a tour of Germany, Austria, and Yugoslavia in support of a single release of "Nuevo Laredo" and "Texas Me," Doug thought that it was a grossly unfair contract, though he had signed it, and that he was not getting the star's attention he deserved.

"Out of the blue," he would later write, "the funky Jewish king of black music . . . called me one day and said, 'T-Bone, you're playing on my team now.' Turns out he'd bought my contract from Mercury. In the process he changed my life. He made it possible for me to assemble one of the most amazing groups of musicians I could ever dream of; he was kind enough to make us feel at home in this big New York City of his; and he was strong enough to push us whenever the music didn't meet his usual standards of excellence."

Doug was never shy about hedging on facts to enhance a good story. Wexler indeed came to town wanting to sign him to Atlantic, but had to ask

Chet Flippo to lead him to Sahm's door, because Doug didn't have a phone. People couldn't just call him up. A *Rolling Stone* article by Stu Werblin maintained that Atlantic's lawyers had tried for a year and a half to figure out how to free him from the Mercury contract, and that Doug, displaying shrewd knowledge of the music business, solved the puzzle. Atlantic would pay Polygram, the European company that owned Mercury, for rights to record and distribute his releases, with Polygram retaining distribution in Germany, Austria, and Switzerland. (Mercury cobbled together another album, *Rough Edges,* from Sir Douglas Quintet outtakes after Doug moved to Atlantic. It was aptly titled, though it did give "Dynamite Woman" its first album exposure.)

Intent on getting all the talent he could out of Austin, Wexler started at the top, as he saw it, in signing Willie Nelson and Doug Sahm. The advances were modest, the rhetoric generous. Wexler was an articulate man given to repetitions of things he'd said or wished he'd said. Of Willie, he would croon in *Texas Monthly:* "The three masters of rubato in our age are Frank Sinatra, Ray Charles, and Willie Nelson, in my opinion. The art of gliding over the meter and extending it until you think they're going to miss the next actual musical demarcation, the next bar—but they always arrive there, at bar one. It's some kind of musical miracle."

He rhapsodized about Doug in the *Austin Chronicle:* "I once made the analogy that Doug was like St. Sebastian—pierced by 1,000 arrows—but instead of blood, talent coming out of every wound. I really regard him as the best musician I ever knew, because of his versatility, and the range of his information and taste."

Never one to waste a good turn of phrase, Wexler later employed distinctly similar language in praise of Jewish musicians he'd known in New Orleans, and Atlantic was not the independent it once had been. Starting in 1969, the Ertegun brothers and Wexler had cashed out handsomely and sold Atlantic into the trend of conglomerate mergers, which produced Warner-Elektra-Atlantic. Though the companies were run separately, people who answered to a higher authority were now looking over the producers' shoulders at profit margins. But Wexler's affection for Doug and his music was genuine; they were constant companions for about six weeks in the fall of 1972. "We were on the same wavelength," Wexler told the *Chronicle*'s Raoul Hernandez, "because he knew I was very attuned to root American music. And I wasn't the usual guy behind a desk with a vest. . . . We both loved Duke and Peacock Records—Bobby 'Blue' Bland, Junior Parker, the Joe Scott Orchestra, which was the backup band for all these great people. Also, what's his name? 'Treat Her Right'? Doug idolized him, Roy Head. He's still playing music from what I understand. Doug had the whole repertoire."

Wexler elaborated to me in our interview, "I was the Jew from New York who knew a lot about western swing. I had a huge collection of it, and not just Bob Wills. I knew the territorial bands like the Pipeliners and the Light Crust Doughboys that Wills started out with; and Adolph Hofner, the Czech and German king of South Texas swing; and Harry Choates, the Cajun fiddler who recorded the country standard 'Draggin' the Bow.' I'd discovered that music when I was going to college in Kansas in the Thirties. And of course Doug knew all about this—he'd started as a prodigy playing the pedal steel in western swing bands. He did the best cover I ever heard of Bob Wills' 'Faded Love.' So the blues and western swing were a big part of it. But you've got a lot of ingredients—jazz, *norteño*, Tex-Mex. He had this *bajo sexto*, also called the *guitarron*, a huge guitar that you see in Mexican bands, and he could play the shit out of it. Also he loved New Orleans music. Bobby Charles was one of his favorite songwriters. Coonass stuff."

Doug was then a thirty-one-year-old hippie with several crash pads in Austin and an ongoing marital wreck in San Antonio, but he was about to embark on a coast-to-coast artistic tear that would have left others panting in exhaustion. Doug never lacked faith in himself, nor ego, but he had figured that his chances of getting signed by Jerry Wexler were about 5,000 to 1. In making the most of it, he characteristically looked out for the interests of others, as well as his own.

In talking up Roy Head, he tried to spark a comeback by one of the stalwarts of Huey Meaux's Tribe Records. Though that suggestion did not bear fruit, Doug took Wexler to watch the young guitarist Stevie Ray Vaughan. "Seeing him one time at the Continental Club was almost an out-of-body experience," said Wexler. He boasted that the next morning he called the director of the Montreaux Jazz Festival in Switzerland. "'You gotta book this musician I'm telling you about. There's no time, I have no tapes, no videos, no nothing—just book him,'" Wexler claimed he said, then continued, "And he did, on my say-

so. And that's where [Vaughan] met David Bowie and Jackson Browne. Bowie took him on the road in his band, and Browne was so taken with him that he gave him free studio time to cut his first album, which [the storied producer] John Hammond took over and released on Columbia." The Montreaux concert and the backing by Bowie and Browne are standard highlights of Vaughan's narrative, but his rapid rise to international fame is not often attributed to a tip to Jerry Wexler by Doug Sahm.

Wexler was interested in several musicians in Austin. But paranoia ran deep in Austin, to borrow the Buffalo Springfield line. The distrust of big record companies was pervasive, and even if it was based on unfair clauses in the

Doug at end of show at Soap Creek in '73, typically bedraggled. Photograph copyright © Burton Wilson, 1997.

contracts, especially on royalties, for many musicians the chip on the shoulder proved counterproductive. Doug also introduced Wexler to Freda and the Firedogs. The bass player and one of the singers and writers was Bobby Earl Smith, a future lawyer and the son of a San Angelo judge. They had a searing lead guitarist, John Reed, who came out of Amarillo and the Lubbock hotbed fueled by Buddy Holly, and the drummer, Freddy Fletcher, was the son of Bobbie Nelson, Willie Nelson's sister and piano player. One night, breaking band rules, Freddy brought onstage for a guest appearance a tall young woman from the Louisiana side of the Sabine River. Marcia Ball played piano and sang blues and country as it was heard in the juke joints that lined the highway between her hometown of St. Charles and the Texas border. She joined up as lead singer, and Freda and the Firedogs thrived as one of Austin's top bands.

The old barkeep and yodeler Kenneth Threadgill was heartbroken when Janis Joplin died in 1970 of a heroin overdose in Los Angeles. Several months later he decided to slow down and give up a regular Sunday night gig at a south Austin bar called the Split Rail. Freda and the Firedogs inherited the gig. Ownership of the sparsely furnished bar had fallen into the hands of genuine, doctrinaire communists who governed the joint by committee and as a result could scarcely agree when to call out the beer trucks to resupply the bar, but the crowds thronged there anyway, especially on Sunday nights. Doug first showed up at the Firedogs' gigs as a spectator. "One night we were taking a break outside, smoking," Bobby Earl recalled. "A guy said, 'There goes Doug Sahm.' I said, '*What?* Doug Sahm was here?' He pointed at this little guy with a cowboy hat, hurrying down the street. The guy said, 'He's been coming out here and watching you a lot.'"

Doug had a career-long knack for cultivating protégés whom he liked and believed he could help. Wexler was crazy about Freda and the Firedogs' live shows, and Doug took him on a long jaunt to watch them record in the East Texas town of Tyler. Wexler had spent some time in Tyler when he was in the army, he was nostalgic about the place and experience, and they had a great time trading stories and watching the band in the small but storied Robin Hood Brian's Recording Studio. The band later recorded an album for Wexler, but it was unreleased for decades because Marcia Ball and others in the band didn't like the Atlantic contract. Then the guitarist John Reed got a draft notice, Marcia got pregnant and moved with her husband out to a place in the country, and a standout band dissolved. "The contract wasn't great," Marcia reflected, looking back, "and we couldn't find a lawyer who could give us any more advice than 'Sign it—it's Jerry Wexler.' They may have been right, though; the label was doing the Austin-Atlantic country thing, and Jerry was sticking his neck out, basically. He had Doug and Tony Joe White and Willie all involved, but he was still sticking his neck out. He wasn't in the best position with Atlantic at the time. It was probably my fault that we drug our feet long enough that he just said, 'Well, I can't work under these circumstances.'"

———

Bobby Earl and Judy Smith were managing a small apartment complex to help pay their bills, and they became good friends of Doug, often providing him with a vacant apartment or an extra room in their unit when he was in town. He wasn't shy about walking through their living room with one of his girlfriends and with brief hi's and bye's taking her straight to bed. He started playing with Freda and the Firedogs at Sunday night gigs at the Split Rail. He waited until the second set when the players and crowd were warmed up. Bobby Earl, who became one of Doug's favorite bass players, reflected on the pervasiveness of sweat in Doug's performances. Doug was a man who hated to be hot, who did not like to perspire. "But Doug would be dripping—his hair would be completely wet. He'd take off his cowboy hat and mop his whole head. That's how I see him at a gig, swabbing up the sweat between songs."

Bobby Earl recalled one night in particular. "He went into that Rolling Stones song 'It's All Over Now.'" It was a Stones cover of a song by a black singer and session guitarist, Bobby Womack, who was then largely known for marrying the wife of his good friend Sam Cooke soon after Cooke was shot and killed in 1964 by a frightened clerk in a seedy Los Angeles hotel. Doug would have been one to know that story. In any case, he went after the song like he was born to be a Rolling Stone, and Bobby Earl was riveted by that night and number at the Split Rail: "He had them dancing on chairs, on tops of tables. It felt like the walls of that place were going to just fly apart. That's when I understood the power of his music."

The Coast-to-Coast All-Star Bands

oug loved Jerry Wexler," said Bill Bentley, who then was writing for an alternative newspaper called the *Austin Sun.* "Jerry was like a father figure to him. Doug couldn't imagine that this deal with Atlantic could turn out to be anything but the right one, the big one." Wexler wanted to make a big splash, releasing two albums in the first year of Doug's associa- tion with Atlantic, and though the contract stipulated that it was with the country division of the label, he gave Doug free rein in deciding whom he would play with and what they would play.

So, with his love and family life in ongoing conflict and irresolution in Austin and San Antonio, he embarked on an eight-month odyssey that would have left many people senseless with travel fatigue—he worked two sessions in San Francisco, two in New York, back for one in San Francisco, then another in New York, and San Francisco again. He started at Wally Heider's studio in San Francisco, taking his frequent drummer George Rains. On two of the early cuts he worked just with Rains. On another he sang and played lead guitar, bass, and keyboards with a rhythm line banged out by Rains and a backing trio of some of the best tenor sax players in the world. Originally from Fort Worth, David "Fathead" Newman, who also played flute on Doug's project, was a leg-

Contact sheet of images from recording sessions in Los Angeles, during the years the band was recorded by Mercury. Photograph copyright © Ron Mesaros.

end who had once been Ray Charles's bandleader; Martin Fierro had been playing with Doug since the *Honkey Blues* days; Mel Martin was a bebop jazz player who, in addition to the sax, excelled on the flute and clarinet. In December Doug went back out with Augie Meyers and enlisted Jerry Garcia on pedal steel and Garcia's friend David Grisman on mandolin. The best of those first San Francisco tracks, a cover of Ned Miller's 1963 country hit "From a Jack to a King," included Garcia and Grisman, but it would not make the cuts in the final editing.

Wexler and Doug had discussed recording at Criteria Studios in Miami, but the producer was getting the impression he needed to spend more time in Atlantic's New York headquarters if he wanted to remain in the power loop. Doug arrived in New York to see friends and bolster his standing with Wexler's peers, and they decided the sessions should take place at the label's legendary studio at 56th and Broadway. Doug had been going up to New York to hang out with Dylan since they met during the original Quintet's run seven years earlier. He liked to tell the story of going to see him one time when Dylan was living on Bleecker Street in Greenwich Village. "He had this wonderful pad," he told Larry Monroe of KUT-FM in Austin, "and I couldn't believe the way he managed the streets. People would go, 'Hey, there's Dylan!' but he just slipped in and out. Anyway, we were in this funky little bar on the East End, and we'd been working on some record, and we had our guitars with us. An old lady was a little drunk, and she said, 'Hey, can you boys play them things? Do you know "San Antonio Rose"?' I looked at Bobby and said, 'Hey, why don't we play for her?' So we cut through 'San Antonio Rose' and two or three Hank Williams's songs, and the bartender comes over and says, 'Hey, you can't do that in here. I don't have a music license, and furthermore you stink. Outta here!' At the time he probably could have been making a million a night, but sometimes you can't give it away."

On this trip, Doug took Dylan out for a long evening and overnight stay at Wexler's beach house on the Bridgehampton Dunes. "If I was relaxed around Bob," Wexler would write with David Ritz in his autobiography *Rhythm and the Blues,* "it was probably because we'd met through our mutual pal Doug Sahm. They played their acoustic guitars and while I beat the conga, waves crashing on the Atlantic, the three of us bonded by music, memories, and the good herb."

Wexler, Doug, and the Atlantic veteran Arif Mardin, who played a fine electric piano, were the producers of *Doug Sahm and Band.* Doug arrived in New York in early October 1972 with his core band of Texans—Augie Meyers (on temporary leave from his Western Head Band) on keyboards, George Rains on drums, Jack Barber on bass and backup vocals, and Rocky Morales on tenor saxophone. Doug also brought along his old crony J. R. Chatwell, who had recently suffered a stroke and couldn't play much on his fiddle, only a little piano. But Wexler considered Chat the Cat one of the greats of western swing and paid him for the sessions. As an eighth birthday present, Shawn Sahm got to ride the train up to New York with Atwood Allen, the beefy and jocular backup guitarist and singer who pumped gas part-time in San Antonio and provided what his dad called "that high Johnny and Jack harmony."

Doug's most exotic import was Flaco Jimenez, who stunned the New Yorkers with his accordion play. Flaco's grandfather had been an old-style *conjunto* and *norteño* player on both sides of the Texas and Mexico border. The styles of play were almost identical, with instrumentation provided by players of a button accordion and the *bajo sexto,* the twelve-string Mexican guitar; the arrangements incorporated the polkas and waltzes played by German settlers in the second half of the nineteenth century. Flaco's dad, Santiago Jimenez, made his first record in 1936. Though new styles of accordion were being developed, he insisted on sticking with the traditional two-row button model. Born in 1936, by age fifteen Flaco led San Antonio's top *conjunto* group, Los Caporales, and played a regular gig on Thursday nights on a local TV station. His playing of *conjunto* was animated and happy, influenced by a style heard in Cajun and zydeco music of Louisiana and southeast Texas. But he felt like nothing was changing or getting better for him. "I was playing the same way I played for years," he said on the syndicated radio program *Roots World.* "I knew there was something out there I didn't know."

What was missing, he went on, was revealed to him by Doug Sahm. "Doug told me: 'You're not supposed to play that simple, traditional *conjunto* music.' There are so many players who stayed in the same crater like my papa did. Doug showed me there were other worlds out there." The result, making a rock-and-roll instrument out of a Tex-Mex accordion, was an entirely new concept in New York.

Contact sheet from
sessions in New York
with Jerry Wexler.
Photos by Wendi
Lombardi. Courtesy
of Shawn Sahm.

Wexler reminisced about putting up Doug and his crew in the Mayflower, a marvelous hotel that used to stand near the southwest corner of Central Park. "He had this gallon jar that he opened up and showed me his precious cargo of tar-ridden buds. He said, 'I never go anyplace without that.' Now people who don't know Doug figured he was on speed, but that was wrong. He was just on a natural high all the time. He had to have a couple of joints in the morning just to get down to equilibrium."

Wexler had recently produced one of his favorite records, *Gumbo*, by Doug's friend Mac Rebennack, "Dr. John." He was enlisted on keyboards for the New Orleans style and sound. Also lined up were Martin Fierro, the tenor sax player on *Honkey Blues* and the first San Francisco sessions of the Atlantic project; the trumpet player Wayne Jackson, one of the famed Memphis Horns; the steel guitarist Charlie Owens, who had played with Willie Nelson and Jerry Lee Lewis; and session veterans Kenny Kosek on fiddle and Willie Bridges on baritone sax. Dylan volunteered for most of the sessions and brought along the superb dobro and bottleneck guitar player David Bromberg. "Dylan was a great fan of Doug's," Wexler told Bill Bentley. "And Dylan was a fan of Willie Nelson, and Dylan was a fan of Dr. John. [Dylan] would wander around and pick up a tambourine, or pick up a brush or a guitar, or go over to the Fender Rhodes. So, one time he puts a few bars of guitar on one of the takes, and as I played it back later in the day, it didn't fit, so I erased it. The next day, Dylan comes in, and he's listening, and he says, 'You took out my guitar.' I said, 'Yeah.' So he goes, 'It stunk, right?'" Wexler said that during a subsequent band break Dylan was hanging out in his office and said, "'Man, I've done the word trip—now I want to do the music trip.'" Drawing on that first acquaintance, Wexler went on to produce three of Dylan's albums, including his controversial pronouncement of born-again Christian faith, *Slow Train Coming*; one song on that album, "Gotta Serve Somebody," won Dylan his first Grammy in 1980.

A great deal of foolishness transpired during the Doug Sahm sessions. Wexler recalled that Bette Midler hung around and got very chummy with the backup vocalist Atwood Allen. The Band's Rick Danko and Garth Hudson showed up to watch, but weren't credited as having played. Elton John dropped by one day. "He was wearing a pair of shoes that had hollowed heels with goldfish swimming in them. Imagine the effect this had on the band. He tells the guys—Rocky [Morales] and Jack [Barber] and all the fellows—he says, 'That's what you have to do now.' And Doug told him, with a straight face, 'Well, if that's the kind of thing you have to do now to make it, we might have to wear dresses.' The band was totally mystified; they didn't know who Elton John was, or could be or might be. He was just this guy with fish swimming in his shoes."

Then there was the day Doug and the other Texans developed an urgent need for Mexican food. No place in New York City would do. Doug insisted, according to his son: "'We need that real, down-home Texas Mexican food, man.' So, Wex gets the company plane fired up, and, you guessed it, the groovers are on their way to Texas to get some real Mexican food. The plane lands at the San Antonio airport. Out comes a station wagon from La Rosa Mexican Restaurant. They load the tacos, beans, enchiladas, etcetera onto the plane, and the boys are on their way back with bellies full of the real stuff. The groove could now resume."

Naturally, all of this created a buzz of curiosity and anticipation in New York. "Everything that goes down here is part of a unit, a continuity," Stu Werblin quoted Doug in *Rolling Stone.* "It's all these different pockets of soul merging from all over the country. Like Mac [Dr. John], he and me are both Sagittarius. He's two weeks older than I am." This was a curious remark, if Werblin quoted him correctly. Doug was a Scorpio, and Rebennack was about fifty weeks older. "And he's stoned New Orleans Bayou," Doug went on, "while I'm stoned Texas country Chicano. And Fathead, well, if you had been here the other night you would have seen him come in and play 'Just Like Tom Thumb's Blues' with Bobby [Dylan]—Fathead playing the guitar. Playing authentic T-Bone Walker lines, and those are the best lines I think you can play. Fathead comes from Texas and brings in that whole other side of soul. Do you see what I'm talking about?"

Part of the difficulty in understanding Doug was that your mind had to register and process as fast as he talked. As previously noted, when the journalist Ed Ward had compiled the liner notes for *Sir Doug's Recording Trip: The Best of the Mercury Years,* Doug conned him into believing he was Lebanese. Since he made the claim in the publicity package for one of his own albums, many subsequent press accounts accepted the Lebanese shtick as gospel. On this occasion he was pulling nobody's leg; he was instead trying to explain how regional and ethnic cultures melded, but he wound up contributing to a growing misperception that he was Mexican American. After all, the first line of one song that emerged from the Atlantic sessions was "Soy Chicano," which in English is "I am Chicano," and in response to some songs recorded in Spanish *Rolling Stone* had lauded him as "Chicano of the Year." Years later, in a survey of successful Mexican American rock musicians, the *New York Times*' John Rockwell claimed that Doug was the one who had enjoyed the longest career run. His birth name, the *Times* stated, was Douglas Saldaña.

Though Doug, the producers, and the players had high hopes for the Atlantic debut, it had the earmarks of one of those all-star jams of dueling egos that almost never work well—the band had two top tenor sax players in Morales and Newman, two keyboard stylists in Dr. John and Augie, two able country fiddlers in Doug and Kosek, and two lead singers of some stubbornness and quirks in Doug and Dylan. But if the record failed, it wasn't because they lazed about, stayed high, and talked about what they might play. In four days they recorded at least thirty tracks that made it to the master reels with very little overdubbing. Wexler laughed that for all of Doug's skill as an arranger and bandleader, he was a trick to manage in the studio. "I remember we were set to do one tune, and inadvertently, as Doug was counting something off, I hit the talk-back and said something out of turn. Well, Doug turns around and says, 'The bird has flown! Blues in B-flat.' He changed the whole thing, and off he went with something else."

Doug made some records in his long career that were truly awful. But he was at the top of his game in the New York sessions of *Doug Sahm and Band*. He and his bandmates didn't pander with one teenybop song, and for whatever it's worth, they caught the bird of the prevailing Austin sound and let it fly better than anyone had at that point, at least in a recording studio.

On the first day they nailed "Poison Love," a rollicking old hillbilly standard often rendered with banjo and mandolin. In Doug's arrangement it showcased Flaco's accordion, Bromberg's dobro, and a wonderful romp by Augie on the piano. Then with Doug and Kosek sawing away on their fiddles they performed "Wallflower," a previously unrecorded Dylan song. In their harmonizing, Doug and Dylan sounded like two drunks bouncing off light poles on a sidewalk after their favorite bar shut down—it was written as a waltz.

That day they also recorded Willie Nelson's "Me and Paul," a wry and mournful song about Willie's feelings of always being picked on as a suspicious character, thanks in part to his sidekick and drummer Paul English, a former Fort Worth burglar who wore a vampire goatee and a red and black velvet cape. Doug's singing on that cut wasn't as strong as on "Wallflower"—his voice sounded tired—but the arrangement was carried by blasts of Wayne Jackson's trumpet, background warbles of Dylan's distinctive harmonica, and a smooth pairing of Augie's piano and Bromberg's dobro. One of the album's surprises was Augie's playing of the piano, for until then he had been known almost exclusively for the Vox organ. In these sessions Dr. John played the organ for the most part, and his contribution was fairly muted in the final mix.

But with all of that going on, "Me and Paul" demonstrated that one goal of the record was to showcase all that Doug could do—he thumped away on his barrel-sized Mexican guitar, the *bajo sexto,* and finished off the song whistling the chorus. They went on to record several blues tracks and gave Jimenez plenty of time to cast his borderlands accordion spell with help from the horn section—the song "Chicano" evoked one of those West Side San Antonio joints where low riders cruise past and the walls are painted aqua. But the country-flavored numbers hold up best.

A couple of years later, Willie would dust off a thirty-year-old Fred Rose song, "Blue Eyes Crying in the Rain," and sing it with such heart that it became his song alone. On the second day of the Atlantic sessions, Doug came near that and faced a more difficult chore, because the song he covered, by Dave Kirby and Glen Martin, was distinctly remembered; Charley Pride had made it a number 1 country hit just two years earlier. "This is a song now about my hometown," Doug announced crisply, and he and Kosek went into a barnyard twin fiddle routine; then Doug lowered the bow and, with the exultant high harmony of Atwood Allen, sang some of the most vivid country lines ever written, among them *"Rain dripping down the neck of my shirt / like I ain't got nothing on . . ."*

"Woo hah!" Doug yelled in exultation as they bridged into a steel solo by Charlie Owens. With all respect for Charley Pride, by the time Doug and his band finished "(Is Anybody Going to) San Antone," artistically if not commercially he owned that hitchhiking and truckstop ode to his hometown. It was not hard to decide that would be the opening track on the record. And on they went, much of it a time-sweep tribute to some of the best American

Thanksgiving Day jam and free concert at the Armadillo, 1972. From left to right: Leon Russell at the piano, Sweet Mary Hattersley of the popular Austin band Greezy Wheels on the fiddle, Grateful Dead bassist Phil Lesh, Jerry Barnet on drums, Jerry Garcia playing pedal steel, and Doug on guitar. Photograph copyright © Burton Wilson, 1997.

songwriters: Bob and John Wills's "Faded Love," Woody Guthrie's "Columbus Stockade," T-Bone Walker's "Papa Ain't Salty," Hank Williams's "Hey Good Lookin'" and "On the Banks of the Old Pontchartrain," Jack Clements's "Miller's Cave," Bobby Charles's "Tennessee Blues," and Atwood Allen's "It's Gonna Be Easy."

For what he thought would be his breakout album, Doug also got to make the call on the cover art. He recruited the artist Gilbert Shelton, one of his Texas pals from the San Francisco days. Shelton had started illustrating in Austin when he was a University of Texas student. He was one of the alleged subversives of the Ghetto tenement identified in the undercover report by the Austin police. Since then he had gained renown in hippie society for a comic book series called *The Furry Freak Brothers.* (He later married a Parisian woman and made his home

there and developed an avid following in France.) For the *Doug Sahm and Band* cover, Shelton caricatured an orchestra of fourteen players: Doug out front, wearing a black cowboy hat and boots and playing a fiddle; Dylan wearing another cowboy hat, knee-patched jeans, and boots, playing an electric guitar; Fathead Newman blowing a sax; Dr. John with a top hat and trim cigar behind a baby grand piano; Flaco Jimenez tapping the toe of one boot while playing his accordion; Augie Meyers poking away on his keyboard; others cavorting to the rear.

Doug returned to Texas for the 1972 holidays in a buoyant mood. The Grateful Dead were coming to Austin for a concert at the municipal auditorium; word went around that Doug's friend Jerry Garcia needed some help scoring some drugs. Austin was known then for its ten-dollar one-ounce lids of Mexican weed, and the transaction was easily arranged. But the musician who provided the service looked at the equipment of the California band—they had two of everything—and the missing finger on one of Garcia's hands and thought, "Jerry Garcia's out of dope? How could that be? Didn't he invent it?"

Jim Franklin, the artist who painted armadillos, was in Tulsa painting a mural in his friend Leon Russell's swimming pool when Russell announced he wanted to go to Austin that night. The Dead were playing their concert, and he'd never seen them before. Joe Nick Patoski wrote in his biography of Willie Nelson that after the Grateful Dead's performance Franklin escorted Russell across the street to the Armadillo World Headquarters and made him comfortable with some of the darlings who liked to hang around. The next day found Doug, Willie, and Leon playing songs for each other in the living room of Willie's apartment. The Armadillo staff quickly put together a Thanksgiving dinner and concert (beef stew and brown rice). They drew 1,500 people and let them in free to watch Russell on piano, the Dead's Garcia on steel guitar and Phil Lesh on bass, an Austin favorite called Sweet Mary Hattersley on fiddle, and Doug playing lead guitar in a four-hour jam. Even on that short notice with those people involved, Doug took over onstage as bandleader. The high point was his rendition of Kris Kristofferson's "Me and Bobby McGee."

After the holidays Doug bore down on the second Atlantic album. He used four outtakes from the New York sessions—"Tennessee Blues," "Ain't That Loving You," "Chicano," and "I'll Be There"—while jettisoning at least a dozen. The imprint of Wexler was much diminished; he didn't choose to join the coast-to-coast caravan. But in San Francisco Doug was not lacking for talent at the mixing board; his friend Dan Healy engineered pieces that included the original "Texas Tornado," which became the title track. With Augie on keyboards, Rains on drums, and Barber on bass, Doug brought in players he'd known in the Bay Area, and he dumped the country-western emphasis in the currents running out toward Alcatraz.

The musicians played with such finesse and restraint that the contrast made *Doug Sahm and Band* sound a little slick. Doug and Wexler reconvened the New York session band in February and March 1973. Wonderfully arranged, "Someday" and "Blue Horizon" had the feel and mood of classy Vegas casino jazz—the singing honored the styles of Frank Sinatra, Dean Martin, Mel Tormé. "Where did he learn to sing like that?" wondered *Texas Monthly*'s Greg Curtis in an incisive review.

Doug then returned to the West Coast for yet another session, but he went back to his roots to bring the album home. He got Louie Ortega, his young friend of Louie and the Lovers, to contribute his voice and guitar to the session that produced the title track. "Texas Tornado" was driven by Rains's drums, the rock guitars, harmony by Ortega and Frank Paredes, a three-piece horn section that had Martin Fierro on tenor sax, as well as a new piano player, Barry Goldberg, who had played at the Newport Folk Festival with Dylan in the first plugged-in set that was famously booed, and had recorded with Leonard

Cohen, Michael Bloomfield, and Stephen Stills, among many others. Goldberg had a deft hand for the old trick of clarissimo, playing all the ivories in one stabbing sweep, which in a rock song can have the effect of a lightning bolt. So what if Doug confused hurricanes with tornadoes in the song's first verse? The chorus and the blistering pace evoked the adrenaline and chaos of people gaping out of a storm cellar at a poisoned cloud as others yelled at them to pull the door down!

But the deadliness of the subject matter was brushed aside by the sheer joyousness of the playing. "Texas Tornado" ranked with "She's About a Mover," "At the Crossroads," and "Adios Mexico," which came out later in his career, as gems of his rock-and-roll songwriting. And many aficionados contend that the *Texas Tornado* album was the best Doug ever recorded. Remarkably, some of the best singing, arranging, and playing didn't make the cut on either Atlantic album. Doug turned a superbly funny country song about a failed love affair on the rhyme *"Now my dear, it is your turn / I'm just tired of getting burned."* His writing over the years was described in many ways, but "poignant" was not a word that often came to mind. But with flourishes of Tex-Mex-style guitar, another song confronted the possibility that hopes soaring so high could end up dashed like all the others—with some guy packing up his guitar case and moving on. *"Sometimes you've got to stop chasing rainbows / and get it together before you cry."* That beautiful song, "Sometimes You've Got to Stop Chasing Rainbows," went unreleased for the rest of his life.

Several outtakes included on the Atlantic-Rhino retrospective *Doug Sahm: The Genuine Texas Groover* are valuable simply because they convey the spirit of those sessions. In "Bobby's Blues," one of the songs recorded in New York, Doug sang snatches of tribute to Bobby "Blue" Bland's "Further On Up the Road" and reserved ample time for his guitar, half-blues, half-jazz, but with ongoing verbal cues he directed and arranged the riffs of the horn players, a solo by his rock-solid bass player Jack Barber, and a glimmering cameo on electric piano by the producer Arif Mardin. "Yeah!" Doug yelled in support of Mardin, laughing. He sang along with a bit of scat as the trumpet player, Wayne Jackson, led them to the close. But the instant they were done, there came this clipped exchange between the man in the booth and Doug on the studio floor.

"Can you do it again so we can record it?" said Wexler.

"Record it . . ."

"We gotta have a beginning, man."

"Beginning!"

"There's no beginning, man."

"No beginning? Man!"

Wexler was utterly mistaken about the piece not being recorded in its entirety. But he went on with some annoyance: "We were just talking, we'd pulled out the instructions . . . Just take it from the top."

"I don't remember what happened," Doug replied. "Get to playing and you're just off in space . . ."

Someone started laughing.

Doug persisted: "Did you get any of it?"

"Try it again, man."

"Did you get *any* of it?"

"Just a little bit at the end, man."

"*Little bit at the end!* Some pretty classic solos there."

Are We a Group?

oug and Willie Nelson got along famously and played on many bills together, but they were a real tandem only in the marketing and pitches
of Jerry Wexler. In April 1973 Willie took his turn in Atlantic's studios in
New York. "I wasn't entirely comfortable at first," Willie told the story.
"Recording in New York was strange. So I went to my hotel and started
pacing. Listening to the radio. Searching for an idea. Finally sat on the
toilet and spotted this sanitary napkin envelope I could write on. I wrote,
'Shotgun Willie sits around in his underwear, biting on a bullet, pulling out all
of his hair.'" The nickname referred to a blast Willie had once fired at an of-
fending son-in-law in Tennessee, and the song piled on political incorrectness
by fondly hailing an old pal in Helotes, Texas, who used to pick up extra money
selling sheets to the Ku Klux Klan. The song was hardly in a league with "Four
Walls," "Crazy," and "The Party's Over," but Willie liked it, and it became the
title track of his declaration of independence from Nashville country.

Rumors spread that George Jones, Leon Russell, and Kris Kristofferson
would play in the *Shotgun Willie* sessions. They didn't show up, but Doug
Sahm and his band did. With Augie taking a turn on acoustic guitar, Doug
played electric lead and sang backup with Waylon Jennings and Jessi Colter on

the rousing Bob Wills song "Stay All Night (Stay a Little Longer)," and Augie, Jack Barber, and George Rains played piano, bass, and drums on another Bob Wills song, "Bubbles in My Beer."

Bobby Earl Smith was in East Lansing, Michigan, for a weeklong gig with Freda and the Firedogs when he called home one night and his wife Judy said that Doug wanted him to come to New York at once. "Doug told me to come on down to the *Shotgun Willie* sessions. It was fun being in New York with Doug. He knew how to do the town. We were walking down the sidewalk outside the Atlantic offices one morning. It was cold and the wind was blowing like hell. I bought a little yarn cap from a street vendor for a dollar to warm my freezing ears. Doug and several of the band boys and I were walking down the street and a little old lady walked up to him and said, 'Are you a group?'

Participants in a conference on the business of music held at the Armadillo in the early Seventies. From left: Doug, BMI-Nashville director Frances Preston, Armadillo co-founder and attorney Mike Tolleson, BMI publicist Russ Sanjek, Willie Nelson, and Willie's then-wife, Connie. Photograph by Ed Malick.

"Doug turned to us and said, 'Did you hear that, boys? She wants to know if we're a group.' Then he turned back to the lady, smiled, and said, 'No, ma'am. We're from Texas.'"

———

When Doug's band went on tour to promote the first Atlantic record, the star guests of the sessions had of course gone back to their own homes, spouses, and children. The manager of Max's Kansas City, a fashionable Manhattan club and restaurant, worried that while Bob Dylan's prominence on the album was a fine endorsement and gesture of friendship, it could also be a beast with horns. Sure enough, the afternoon before Doug and his touring band opened at the club on Park Avenue, a large TV crew from one of the New York stations set up their cameras and watched the musicians rehearse. The club's manager recalled, "After the sound check one of them asked, 'Where's Dylan?' I told them Dylan wasn't booked here this week, and they got very mad." Uninterested in Doug Sahm, they loaded up their gear and went back to the station.

After all the hard work, high hopes, and chasing of rainbows the response to *Doug Sahm and Band* was a heartbreaker. In May 1973 a professed fan of the Quintet's music blistered Doug in *Fusion* magazine for even pursuing the new project: "Doug Sahm is hardly the kind of performer who had to feel like he had to bring a bunch of famous names with him in order to get people to listen to his next record. But either he did feel that way, or he has a bunch of lame-ass friends. . . . The result is by no means a gaudy display of superstar egomania, but rather a testimony to the fact that some great musicians and personalities can get together and make music which is totally colorless, mindless, and gutless. Oatmeal."

Few reviews of the first album were that harsh, but the praise was tepid. *Doug Sahm and Band* proved to be one of those projects in which first reviews and poor sales reports dictated conventional wisdom about its artistic merit; it sat in neglect for decades before listeners rediscovered it or heard it for the first time and started giving it the glowing marks it deserves. Of course, it would have been hard for any record to measure up to the jive that the rock press lavished on the New York sessions. The same versatility and range that attracted Wexler worked against Doug in marketing. "The problem with Doug," he told the *Austin Chronicle*'s Raoul Hernandez, "was you had this river. What are you

gonna bottle and sell?" Wexler told me, "The record generated very little enthusiasm inside the company. We didn't have a single that we could get played on
the radio. We had no hit. And as I often told Doug, a producer can scream at the
promotion people all he wants, but if their hearts aren't into it, they just aren't."

———

Though Doug could hope the jury was still out on *Texas Tornado,* he couldn't fool
himself about the state of his marriage. Violet was starting a new life with this
guy she met through the law office; she no longer wanted him around. Doug
and Violet had found a suitable rent house in Balcones Heights, a onetime
suburb that had been surrounded by the sprawl of San Antonio. Doug's car at
the time was an Oldsmobile Cutlass with distinctive gold and black California
tags. "Cops in Balcones Heights most definitely knew who he was," said
Shawn. "They were always pulling him over in traffic, and one night they came
to the house saying they were looking for stolen property. We were crying,
'Dad, what's going on?'" The cops went straight to his sock drawer, trying without any luck to find his stash. And as if Doug didn't have enough troubles, the
trumpet player of his road band got arrested on some vague charge in the rest-
room of a local service station. Then his great friend and star sax player Rocky
Morales bonked his car into another vehicle that belonged to a San Antonio
cop—like the trumpet player he also went to jail.

One afternoon in May George Rains flew from San Francisco to San
Antonio. His drums hadn't arrived with him, which was irritating, but Doug
was there waiting with his old friend J. R. Chatwell, the western-swing fiddler
and hipster. The following summary of their evening's surprise turn is adapted
from subsequent court testimony and one of George Rains's essays on the
period. As they chattered, Doug drove straight to La Rosa Mexican Restaurant,
the hangout to which, eight months earlier, Wexler had flown the band to
satisfy their hunger for tacos and quesadillas during the high-rolling Atlantic
sessions in New York. The restaurant was noisy and lively, its owners enjoying
a good night. The three of them were talking and eating when a uniformed cop
on the Balcones Heights force walked in and started asking restaurant staff
and diners who owned the Oldsmobile Cutlass with California license plates.

Doug stood up and said, "What's the problem?"

"No problem," said the officer, who stepped back and held the glass door open. "Just step outside, sir."

The café suddenly went very quiet, and people stared at Rains and Chatwell. The drummer looked outside and with a jolt of alarm saw that several cops had Doug bent over the hood of his Olds, and they were handcuffing him. With a rush that he later compared to an epiphany, Rains foresaw that they were all going to be arrested. He had a couple of joints in his pack of cigarettes. Their table was shoved up against a wall. Rains claimed that he was hunched over trying to get them out of the pack and toss them on the darkened floor, when Chatwell touched his hands and muttered, "Here, take this."

Take it? Doug often joked that J. R. slipped out of his house after supper and in his Hush Puppies cruised to a secret cache of pot that put a sweet different light on an evening. But now in the panic of the moment, Rains claimed, the old-timer wanted him to take a couple of joints wrapped in a paper napkin off his hands.

Doug sporting his famous police-inflicted shiner with his kids and *Rolling Stone* writer Chet Flippo and wife. Photo courtesy of Shawn Sahm.

Through the door one of the cops noticed their suspicious postures and behavior. Soon they were also outside, with their hands cuffed behind them. Doug twisted, scuffled, and carried on a dialogue with the cops, who called the musician by name and seemed to be enjoying the contretemps. One grabbed a fistful of Doug's hair and slammed him hard, face-first, against the hood of his Cutlass.

"Didn't bother Doug," recalled Rains. "He kept right on talking. 'You pig-fucking cocksuckers.' Stuff like that."

A grinning officer leaned over and proposed to Doug: "How 'bout we take those cuffs off and you just start runnin'? How 'bout we do that, hippie?"

"Fuck you," Doug replied.

Rains thought this was getting way out of hand. As the cops confiscated his Vicks Inhaler as possible narcotics paraphernalia Rains suggested to Doug that if he didn't calm down there was an excellent chance the cops would either kick him quiet or shoot him.

Rains said it was like a lightbulb came on inside Doug's head. He hadn't thought it that far through. Doug abruptly stopped moving and said not one more word. Chatwell interjected, "Listen here, I just got over a stroke and my left arm don't work so good. Could you loosen these handcuffs just a little?"

"Shut up!" a cop yelled.

"Yes sir!"

Convinced by the pot in the others' possession that they had probable cause, the police ransacked Doug's car, throwing out tapes and clothes and cowboy hats, and in the rough handling his prized antique fiddle fell out of its case and snapped in two when it hit the ground. Rains and Chatwell were charged with possession of marijuana, but the cops' search of Doug's person and car produced nothing. An officer shined a flashlight in Doug's face and noted that one of his eyes was particularly bloodshot (from having his face banged hard on the car). They arrested Doug for public intoxication. Rains said that as the cops were preparing to take them to jail, a waitress came outside and asked if these people could first be made to pay the bill for their beers and enchiladas.

Welcome home, whirlwind. Now why is it they call you "Sir"?

Soap Creek

Doug was an outlaw only in his choice and sharing of intoxicants, but he definitely had a dim view of cops. In this latest and most dangerous episode the officers served on the force of Balcones Heights, not San Antonio. Dressed in cowboy attire at the misdemeanor trial, which convened in June 1973, the lead officer testified that he "placed Sahm's head against the car because it seemed to me that he had a rabbit in his blood and police officers don't like subjects who might run." (The officer talked like he'd been watching the movie *Cool Hand Luke* and admired the style and delivery of Strother Martin, who played the warden.) He volunteered to the judge his opinion that Doug was "nutty as a fruitcake."

The judge threw out the charge of public intoxication for lack of probable cause. "It's my show now!" Doug yelled at the cop outside the courthouse. But the violin that the police had shattered was a seventy-year-old antique. He had watched them manhandle and humiliate an ailing friend who was nearly sixty years old. In the wake of all the poor and glaring publicity, the phone company informed Doug that he was no longer an appropriate candidate for its service. The person most affected by the turmoil, of course, was his estranged wife. Doug sued the police and municipality of Balcones Heights for $450,000, but his conduct that night meant his chances of winning a judgment were nil. He wore an ugly shiner that took a long time to go away.

The violent run-in with cops outside Doug's favorite hometown café wasn't the causal factor in his divorce from Violet, but it was a catalyst. When they at last gave up their erratic attempts to reconcile, Doug was angry and bitter and felt betrayed. They had been barely old enough to buy a bottle of beer legally when they married, and as time went on they discovered they wanted very different things in life. The divorce was so hard on both of them that they let the house and acreage in Prunedale go to the IRS to pay off back taxes; Doug's only real estate purchase would have been worth a fortune if he and Violet had been able to separate their business sense from their emotions and hang onto that vestige of the wild years in California.

Doug went on loving San Antonio as a stage for world-class music and a reservoir of treasured memories, but he never again felt quite the same about the city's streets and the people who ruled them. When he came back home, he was looking for someplace in Texas that was peaceful and tolerant of his personality and way of life. Doug was a city guy, born and raised; living out in the country was not an option for him. With his marriage over and his hometown ruled out, Austin was the only contender.

"Groovers Paradise": the notion struck him one day when he saw some hippies poking around a downtown junkyard called Snooper's Paradise, and he wrote a song about the inherent freedoms of the town. For several years, he believed his myth was true.

A fault line and limestone escarpment had thrust up rugged hills and divided Austin from rolling savanna to the east and gave the city much of its striking physical character, but the hills had been badly overgrazed when they were ranchland prairie, which set the voracious water-sucking junipers loose and made the Hill Country terrain look more verdant than it normally is. Doug found a two-story brick mansion in Westlake Hills, which was then a suburb occupied by University of Texas professors, cedar choppers, and numerous dope dealers. The dense brakes of nettlesome trees, which most folks called cedar, ensured his privacy, but from his hilltop he had a long, fine view of Austin's skyline, which was then dominated by the pink granite state capitol and a university tower that was lighted orange on nights when the Longhorn

teams won. (One August afternoon in 1966, Charles Whitman, an engineering student and former marine, altar boy, and Eagle Scout, demonstrated that the deck around the tower's clocks made an excellent sniper's roost. He killed six-teen people and wounded thirty-two more before Austin policemen finally got up the stairs and killed him. He was kept ducking and denied more victims by a freelance posse snooping into range and taking potshots with hunting rifles. Austin was nobody's paradise that day.)

On matters of upkeep the mansion was something of a wreck. The land-lord wanted little to do with the house, and the rent he charged Doug was a bargain. He had plenty of room for friends and his children when they came to visit. And a short stroll down the slope was a seedy-looking, recently opened L-shaped joint called Soap Creek Saloon. A couple named Carlyne Majer and George Majewski were its owners and bookers of the musicians. She was dark-haired and pretty, and had a no-nonsense air conducting business. He was a tall, good-natured hippie of such homely visage that it made him an Austin celebrity; for several years the bar's festivities included a spirited George Majewski Lookalike Contest. The bar and Doug's house sat far back among

The end of a hot night at Soap Creek. At the far left is bass player Jack Barber. Rocky Morales is on saxophone. Doug is seated and beaming at his children Shandon and Dawn. Photograph copyright © Burton Wilson, 1997.

the cedars at the end of an unpaved caliche road with potholes big enough to break axles. A hard rain turned the white dust into a gloppy mess. Soap Creek would survive in three more locations after upscale development along Bee Cave Road squeezed it out of Westlake Hills (one of them the site of the storied Skyline Country Club, where the Band once played, according to guitarist Robbie Robertson, with a one-armed go-go dancer, and Little Doug Sahm had perched for a photo in the bony lap of Hank Williams). The original Soap Creek Saloon was as essential to Austin's ascendance as a music capital as the Armadillo World Headquarters.

Doug and most Austin musicians were delighted to play both places, but the owners and some habitués of Soap Creek had a prickly attitude toward the Armadillo and the people who ran it. Soap Creek was smaller than the Armadillo, it was easier to watch the musicians in close proximity, and the state had just changed the law enabling bars in communities that approved the option to sell liquor. The directors of the Armadillo stuck with beer and cheap wine, while the owners of Soap Creek scrounged up enough money to pay for the liquor license. At a panel put on long after both enterprises had passed out of existence, Carlyne Majer contended, "The Armadillo's focus was on booking major touring acts. We wanted to provide a home to local artists, and our shows encompassed blues and country and roots rock." Eddie Wilson and the other Armadillos took pride in being able to book acts like Frank Zappa, Van Morrison, and the emerging Bruce Springsteen, but Wilson snorted with exasperation on hearing gripes that they discriminated against local bands and that they booked cosmic cowboys to the exclusion of others. It was hard to find a night when an Austin band wasn't on the bill. But Soap Creek was the un-Cola of Austin music venues. Cosmic cowboys who didn't behave could find themselves thrown out in the parking lot and their hats twirled after them. Soap Creek regulars spent many nights chasing their beers with cheap tequila and listening to a blues band called Paul Ray and the Cobras, whose then-obscure lead guitarist was a Dallas exile named Stevie Ray Vaughan.

Speedy Sparks was one of the Soap Creek bartenders and doormen. He had grown up in Houston, where he played bass in teen garage bands, and while attending college in East Texas, he had gone to Shreveport one night to watch the Sir Douglas Quintet in their Beatle boots phase. Not long after that, Speedy got drafted, and he spent part of his army tour in Okinawa. "I'd go buy a *Rolling*

Stone, and it seemed like every other issue had a big story about Doug Sahm. I knew about 'She's About a Mover' and 'Mendocino,' but I thought, man, they sure must like him. We weren't hearing any hits from him on the radio now."

After his discharge Speedy landed in Austin in 1972, crashing in apartments of friends who had come to the university and, like thousands of others, had not moved on. He convinced Soap Creek's owners that he knew how to mix drinks. "I was a real lousy bartender," he said. "When Doug moved next door, he would come down for an afternoon beer and stop to talk, and that's how I got to know him."

He laughed, recalling Doug's first gig. "He was into his scene with the West Side Horns then. They camped there two days, with Rocky Morales drink-

Doug at the mansion above Soap Creek with his dog Bingo and John Reed, far left. Among the Latino friends and musicians is San Antonio's Frank Rodarte, far right. Photo courtesy of Shawn Sahm.

ing and charging it up on the bar tab. That's when I met Shawn, who was about eight years old. When they got up to play that night, everybody realized this was not the typical Austin band. There wasn't one hippie on the stage, not really. They were post-beatnik era. The first song Doug played at Soap Creek was 'Wolverton Mountain'"—the 1962 hit by Claude King, one of Doug's country favorites. "Then they broke into a Bobby 'Blue' Bland song, and the crowd reaction was—*okay!* Where have they been?" The cast would change, except for the leader, but Soap Creek Saloon had just gained a new house band.

"What got me," Speedy said of the Austin music scene, "was that guys like Alvin Crow and Ray Benson and even Doug were playing Bob Wills songs. Grandpa music! From a bunch of young guys who still had all their Beatles and Rolling Stones and blues and soul records! I'm thinking, 'What the hell are they playing *that* for?' I didn't quite get it at first."

In a wide-ranging interview by Bill Bentley for the *Austin Sun,* Doug reflected on the split personalities of his music and his crowds of friends. When Bentley asked him if he was planning to record more country material, he answered, "Sure, I don't ever like to stay in one bag. I like to do it all. A lot of people think I'm a cosmic cowboy. Well, maybe so, but I'm a rocker too and I want to be Austin's rocker. I have a lot of people around me that can't stand country music." Bentley mused that Austin might get typecast by its country vogue in a way that hurt the prospects of its musicians. Doug said, "Well, people have opinions but remember: Texans aren't pushovers. They know there's a whole spectrum and they know I'm a man of many worlds. For instance, I'm part of Willie Nelson's world and I love it but at the same time, I'm part of the Grateful Dead's world. And those two worlds just aren't the same world. One night I might be playing twin fiddles at the Broken Spoke and the next night I'll be down at Antone's playing the blues. In that way Texas is a paradise, because all that music is here."

"The people who hung out at Soap Creek," reminisced Speedy Sparks, "had gleams in their eyes like it was some kind of Masonic ritual. They were an enlightenment committee or something. In the mid-Sixties, when Doug came along, that was the day when rock-and-roll stars were royalty. Doug had the credentials; he was royalty. In '73 Doug was the one around here, not Willie. I knew Willie had written some hit country songs, but they were, hell, country.

Willie used to come out and just watch Doug. He was trying to figure out how to get that rock-and-roll crowd. One afternoon Doug was having a beer and talking to Willie and Johnny Winter. They were all huddled at a table. Doug said, 'You know what we oughta do? We oughta come out here and jam to-night and play.' It wasn't thirty minutes until the place started getting packed. They didn't start for another hour and a half, but word of it just flew around. People wanted to see that, and Doug was the one who got it together."

———

One night in early 1974, Doug put together his most celebrated gig at Soap Creek Saloon. He had been thrilled to play in San Antonio with Freddy Fender in the late Fifties, he often sang "Wasted Days and Wasted Nights" in his gigs, and in 1971, on *The Return of Doug Saldaña,* he had covered it with the rever-ential introduction: "This is a song written by the great Freddy Fender. Freddy, this is for you, wherever you are."

Hardly anybody in the music business knew where he was. Fender had served two and a half years in the sweltering fields of Angola on his marijuana conviction, and a condition of his parole was that he avoid places that served alcoholic beverages. He laid low for a while in New Orleans, soaking up Cajun music and playing in Louisiana and Texas hellholes, as he put it, that didn't advertise that they had music. Fender later moved to Corpus Christi, where he again went by his birth name, Baldemar Huerta. He worked as a mechanic, took some classes in social work at Del Mar Junior College, and played on weekends in cantinas and icehouses, if at all. He had likely forgotten his gringo admirer who played with him on a bill or two fifteen years earlier.

But Doug was persistent. With the help of Huey Meaux, he tracked Fender down and persuaded him to come to Austin and play a headliner with him at Soap Creek Saloon. Fender showed up in a fringed leather vest and started off playing like it was a gig in a hotel lounge. He was clearly nervous and uncertain who these people were and where he'd landed. Doug and his band joined him in the second set and with some especially strong sax play by Morales, they coaxed him out of his fit of nerves and into the fluid voice that first made him known as El Bebop Kid, the Mexican Elvis. Fender leaned over the instrument that gave him his performance name and showed that he could play electric guitar with just about anybody.

Huey Meaux won Fender's confidence following that gig—some said, because they were fellow ex-cons—and took over his management. The same year that Doug lured him back into public life at Soap Creek, Fender's "Before the Next Teardrop Falls" became the first single to reach number 1 on both the pop and country-western charts of *Billboard*. The industry trade magazine went on to proclaim it the fourth-hottest song of 1975. Soon Fender was singing on the Johnny Carson show. A rerecording of "Wasted Days and Wasted Nights" reached the top ten on the pop charts. On the album version, Fender returned the favor by saying the song was "dedicated to my soul partner, wherever he is, Doug Sahm." Fender went on to chart twenty-one country hits over the next eight years. Doug's gesture completely revived a downcast man's career.

Doug tried just as hard to help Roky Erickson. He put up his own money in support of the troubled rocker who had amazed him with his radio hit "You're Gonna Miss Me" and the 13th Floor Elevators' Avalon Ballroom shows in San Francisco in 1966. Erickson was out of prison by 1975 but no less mentally ill and hooked on drugs. He could still play up a blaze on the electric guitar; one could see why he had been a boy wonder a decade earlier. He formed a new band called Blieb Alien whose first name was an anagrammatic reference to the Bible; the two words were allegedly translated in German as "Remain Alone." Many people in Austin were supportive of Erickson in friendly and protective ways, but his gigs were few and far between.

In the summer of 1975 Doug took Erickson and his players to Odyssey Studios in Austin and handed over a few hundred dollars to record a demo tape that might help get Erickson some bookings in the clubs. The partners of the little studio had a standing joke that they could cut records and have them on the street the next day. On hearing Doug's monologue as producer, they realized it was no joke to him. He brought some of his famous weed to help things along. As it had been on the records of the Elevators, Erickson's run-and-gun singing voice managed to be both a tenor and a growl, and his lyrics paid homage to old horror and science fiction movies. "*Two headed dog, two headed dog / I've been working in the prison with a two headed dog*," he belted out on the A side. Doug lost money on "(Red Temple Prayer) Two Headed Dog" and "Starry Eyes" and probably knew that he would. Erickson eventually gained a measure of cautious lucidity and made a comeback with the help and care of his brother, Sumner.

Erickson was often a guest at Doug's mansion off Bee Cave. "We all loved Roky," said Shawn. "But then a big thunderstorm would come up, and Roky would be directing it with all these sound effects. The climax was when lightning struck close by. He clapped his hands one time, very loud. It was like he commanded the thunder. We really thought he was making it happen. Pop was yelling, 'Roky, stop it, you're scaring the kids!'"

Dawn, Shawn, and Shandon stayed with their dad on weekends and during summer vacations, visits that sometimes were arranged on the spur of a moment. Dawn told me, "We thought that house was haunted, so we were very glad to go down to Soap Creek, whether Dad was playing that night or not. We'd stake out these sofas beside the bar and hang out with a guy named Billy Bob, who worked the door. Shandon used to irk guys by swiping quarters they put on the pool table to challenge winners of the games. I thought I wanted to be an actress, but what did I know about music? Keith Ferguson played bass for the Fabulous Thunderbirds"—a stalwart Austin blues and rock band led by the singer and harmonica player Kim Wilson and guitarist Jimmie Vaughan, Stevie Ray's older brother. "One time Dad had some gigs lined up and didn't

Roky Erickson, bearded, center, in comeback facilitated by Doug. Behind Roky is record producer Bill Beatley (in glasses). Photo courtesy of Shawn Sahm.

have a bass player for the band, so he just hired Keith at Soap Creek and told him to come along. Keith was very nervous about it, saying Dad was such a giant, such a pro. I spouted off and gave him this inspirational lecture—'You are just as good as anybody, you can play with anyone.' I found out later that he talked for years about how much that meant to him."

Doug's expansive new home and the beer joint down the hill exposed his children to a great deal more of his lifestyle (Speedy Sparks, they now joke, provided the Sahm kids' day care). "I feel like I grew up in Soap Creek Saloon," Shawn said. "They had this moth-eaten old sofa, and, boy, I made that my territory. I got my first performance bucks doing a Cheech and Chong routine during band breaks. Dawn and I were little scammers. We'd try to charge people for parking when it was obvious it was free.

"Pop's house, well, let's just say he had his own way of doing things. If we'd come along a few years later, the Department of Child Protective Services would have been all over that scene. Papers and junk were piled up everywhere. There was always a mess in the kitchen, and there were rats as big as cats. A rat was always dying in the walls, and the smell was awful. Pop would say, 'All right, kids, first one that finds the rat gets five dollars.'"

"I was just a little kid," Shandon recalled those years. "One time Dad had some gig out in L.A. and he took us with him. We were at a hotel and playing around the pool." The hotel was the Tropicana, famous for its clientele of rock musicians, and Doug quickly found some company of adults who amused and distracted him. A man working around the hotel walked by the pool, grinned

Dawn and Shandon Sahm at the Armadillo, Thanksgiving, 1972. Doug is in the background stroking his chin. Photograph copyright © Burton Wilson, 1972.

at the scampering kids, and playfully picked up Shandon and tossed him in the deep end. Shawn cried out in dismay that Shandon couldn't swim, then jumped in after him. Shawn thought his fiercely struggling little brother was going to drown them both before they reached the shallow end. Shandon said, "I was three years old. Shawn saved my life."

The kids had a fairly conventional life in San Antonio with their mother and school and friends, but on the frequent occasions they went to Austin to stay with their dad it was like they had joined an exotic campout. "I remember a lot of going to sleep on sofas," said Shandon. "Dad would pick me up and carry me home from Soap Creek or to the car from houses of his girlfriends. He always had lots of girlfriends. I remember a few times when one would start up the stairs and he'd be up in his bedroom with another one. We'd stare at each other and try not to laugh, wondering what was going to happen. I had a friend named Roland that I played with all the time. Dad would load us up in his car and take us swimming at Barton Springs. Nights at Soap Creek, I was always trying to get quarters from people so I could play pinball. One time when Dad had the gig I was chewing gum and popped a filling out of my tooth. I went up and poked him in the leg—in the middle of a set, between songs!—and showed him part of a tooth in my hand. Freaked him out, he got all jangly, the way he would."

Shandon laughed. "I got a little older and had a skateboard. There was this dirt lane from Soap Creek to Dad's house, and a steep paved lane down to Bee Cave Road, which was a busy street, even back then. One day he said, 'Skate down the hill, son, and I'll catch you.' He jogged down the hill, and was down there with his arms spread like he was going to make a tackle in football or something. By the time I got down there I was flying, and—*bam!*—both of us went head over heels. He said, 'What a dumb idea! If I'd missed you, you would have been run over.'"

"Doug Sahm at Wille's."
Drawing by Shawn
Sahm, age 10.

Doug in a moment of vanity preparing for a gig during the "Groovers Paradise" years. Photo courtesy of Shawn Sahm.

Groovers Paradise

Doug had a conversational tic. He'd be talking to someone, anyone, and put his hand beside his mouth, as if he were confiding a great secret. One time he was coming off the stage of the Austin Continental Club after a performance and in this manner confided to a young woman who was quite a fine blues singer in her own right: "I gave myself chills." He rarely had a poor opinion of himself. Eddie Wilson, the Armadillo cofounder and driving force, recalled one Sunday afternoon when he and Doug were having lunch together at one of Austin's Night Hawk restaurants. Doug launched into some opinions and speculations about pro football, except that time he put his hand on the side of his mouth so that, if anything, it projected his insults toward some black guys who were sitting nearby and were sure to take offense. On TV screens positioned about the room the hallowed Dallas Cowboys were playing, and Doug was passing on scuttlebutt that several of the team's black stars were queers. Eddie figured Doug was lucky one of those fans didn't hang him upside down and squash his face in his gravy, and Eddie would have been disposed to just clear out, personally. That was not the only time Doug pulled a stunt like that; he'd stop at some beer joint in the middle of nowhere and happily start needling the rednecks about America's Team as his children squirmed. He never demonstrated that he cared much of anything about football. But for whatever reason, he despised the Cowboys. It was one of his calling cards.

Baseball was different—baseball was a passion. Hitting the road to big league spring training camps and following the Chicago Cubs to the second division every September did not diminish his appetite for ball games. He had pals scattered around the country whose common bond was a love of ball games, far more than music. A softball contest with a San Antonio team led to a close friendship with a civil service worker and pitcher named John Colvillo, who played for a team that won a state championship. Doug was also attached to him because he worked at Kelly Air Force Base, as his dad the elder Vic Sahm had.

Doug nicknamed him "Koufax," after the great Dodgers pitcher Sandy Koufax, and often made a 170-mile round-trip to watch the team play. "One time the Houston Astros and Detroit Tigers played a spring training game on our minor league field," Koufax chortled, "and Doug had an assignment with some little music magazine to cover the game. He called me and said, 'Come on, I've got press credentials.' These sportswriters all had on Dockers and knit shirts and were typing away on laptops. They were slipping looks at Doug in his wild hippie garb, scribbling away on a tablet, spouting statistics about every player. All of a sudden he says, 'It's hot in here! Where's the thermostat?' These sportswriters are going, 'Who *is* this guy?' He tears out of there, then there's this *thump*, the lights flicker in the whole park, and he comes back mission accomplished, one guy who knows how to turn the AC down."

Doug was not just a spectator at the softball games. He was hardly a jock. He didn't smoke tobacco or drink anything that contained more alcohol than beer, but he also seldom worked out—he would jog in place for a few minutes, pull up winded, and tell his kids he had just chugged the equivalent of six miles. But the Austin summer leagues had never experienced a player-coach like him.

His slow-pitch teams were made up of young above-average athletes, and he was the man on the mound. The first sponsor was a newly founded restaurant called Jeffrey's that quickly gained a reputation as the city's best. "We were working so hard in those years just trying to stay open," said owner Ron Weiss, who ran the restaurant with his wife Peggy, "that I didn't get to see them play very often. But they had some fellows who were really good. Like they had this guy one year who had recently been a starting quarterback for the University of Texas.

"But it was Doug's team, so they had a zany edge. One time I watched them in a league playoff game on Halloween. All of our guys showed up in these ridiculous bumblebee costumes. Which made the other team furious. So they start the game, and Doug's guy is leading off. He gets what should have been a single but instead runs directly from home plate to third base! Those other guys are so mad they can't even spit, and they fall apart on the field. Doug's team pours it on, beats them by ten or fifteen runs wearing the bumble-bee suits."

Another time, he showed up for a game in a Zorro costume. A cautious ump told him, "Sir, you're going to have to leave that sword on the bench." When he was living in the hilltop mansion, Soap Creek Saloon became the ball team's logical sponsor. The Soap Creek Bombers were hippies who could play. Despite their youth and skill, none of them competed with more intensity than the coach. Shawn's games of catch with his dad consisted of holding his glove without moving while Doug lobbed softballs, trying to plop them down precisely and master his control. During one game somebody winged Doug with a hard line drive back at the mound. Accompanied by Shawn, he went to a sport-

Doug with his San Antonio softball chum John Colvillo, whom he nicknamed "Koufax" for his pitching talent. Photo courtesy of Shawn Sahm.

ing goods store and outfitted himself in catcher's equipment—shin and knee guards, chest guard, and mask. "I'll never forget watching him admire himself in a mirror at the store. He turned both directions, looked over his shoulder, and then he started going through his pitching motion in front of the mirror. Before he paid for all that protective gear he wanted to be sure it didn't ruin his delivery." Doug went out and played in the catcher's armor. The guys who played in that league were merciless. The other team booed and jeered him until their throats gave out.

Always, it seems, Doug endured no paucity of women. He was not a homely man, but neither was he a rock star blessed with the looks of, say, his pal in the Band, Rick Danko. But his gigs at Soap Creek were remarkable for the number of loosely dressed, pleasantly scented, very attractive young women dancing and putting on a show right up against the stage. This story involving Doug might be apocryphal, but most likely it's not. An Austin guitar player and friend of Doug rolls up to the house to see him one Saturday morning, believing he's expected. The visitor sees the cars, knocks on the door, pokes around for a couple of minutes, and finally yells, "Hey, Doug! *Doug!* You in there?"

Doug opens a window upstairs, pokes his head out, and tells his friend that he's tied up doing something right now, to go on inside and make himself at home, he'll be down in a minute. The friend opens the door and walks into the living room, where he finds a guy sitting on a sofa and playing a guitar while watching the morning cartoons. He nods and mumbles something and continues playing. He's not just doing this in a vacant-minded way. He's got the TV's sound turned down, he's playing a score for the images, and it works musically in some strange way. The Austin guitar player watches him doing this for a few moments, along with the cartoons' colored jumble of movement, and then he eyes the other fellow again. Other guitars are lined up around the room. Doug's friend picks one up, quickly makes sure it's tuned, and starts playing, too. Their heads bob slightly as they work in together. The Austin guy glances at the other one and finally says, "You look a lot like . . . what's that guy's name . . . Dylan. Bob Dylan."

"Right," mumbles the other. "I'm Dylan."

What does this story say about Doug? He's up there taking his time making love to the wife of the good friend he told to make himself at home downstairs.

—

One part of Doug chilled out when he was off the road, enjoying a smoke in his hammock and the parade of women friends through his mansion. He had been motivated by nothing but generosity in facilitating the comebacks of Freddy Fender and Roky Erickson and doing all he could to help Louie and the Lovers and Freda and the Firedogs. But anyone with as much talent and ego as Doug had to be frustrated. The sales reports for *Texas Tornado* came back even worse than those for *Doug Sahm and Band.* One part of him was common man, the Musical Mayor of Austin. Another was almost frantic to reclaim his international stature as a rock-and-roll star. The only way to do that was to score new hits and claw his way back up the charts, but his dream deal with Atlantic was falling apart. He had written a telling song a few years earlier called "Me and My Destiny." At this point in his life, he wasn't in control of it.

Willie Nelson's *Shotgun Willie* had created a large stir in Texas, but like *Doug Sahm and Band* it bombed by Atlantic's standards. Willie embarked on an end run on his next recording, a story album about a failed marriage called *Phases and Stages.* Though it got caught up in interoffice Atlantic wrangles that infuriated Wexler, *Phases and Stages,* released in March 1974, was a much better album than *Shotgun Willie.* One of its cuts, a standard of his roadhouse repertoire called "Bloody Mary Morning," rose to number 17 on *Billboard*'s country chart. Willie also recorded a duet single with Tracy Nelson (no relation), the big-voiced rock singer brought to light in San Francisco by Doug's old friend Travis Rivers and the Texan-loaded band Mother Earth. "After the Fire Is Gone" likewise climbed to number 17, but neither of those promising signs convinced the Atlantic executives in New York. In September Atlantic decided to shut down its country-western experiment. Wexler told Joe Nick Patoski that he protested to the Ertegun brothers, "'You can't do this. We've got Willie Nelson now.' The response was 'Willie who? Go ahead and close it.'" Wexler did as he was ordered, and he resigned from Atlantic a few months later. Despite all his love for the music and the bonhomie, he was able to champion his Texas artists for only a year and a half.

"Doug didn't hold it against Jerry," Bill Bentley said, "but he really felt burned by the experience with Atlantic." Yet he signed with a sister label, Warner—it was better than having no contract at all. Wexler also landed with Warner for

a while, though never again as Doug's producer. He remained a friend and effusive fan of Willie and Doug, and over the years he continued to boost some Austin musicians, coproducing Lou Ann Barton's debut *Old Enough* and hiring the Fabulous Thunderbirds to back up Carlos Santana on his album *Havana*.

On Doug's first record for Warner, he all but wallowed in Austin mystique. Augie had his own act going in the clubs with the Western Head Band, and Doug took a break from trying to keep his pals with the West Side Horns together and paid. In the new band, which he called the Tex-Mex Trip, the only one of his San Antonio cohorts was Frank Rodarte, an alto and tenor sax and flute player. Doug hired Link Davis, Jr., a Port Arthur native who played various horns, keyboards, and fiddle. Doug credited him on the album's liner notes for its "cosmic Cajun trips." All the other players were California imports. During the heady touring days with the Quintet he had become friends with members of the hugely commercial roots rock band Creedence Clearwater Revival, and now their drummer, Doug Clifford, and bass guitar player, Stu Cook, became the rhythm section of the Tex-Mex Trip. They recommended other session players, and along with Russ Gary, Creedence Clearwater's studio engineer, they coproduced Doug's Warner debut.

The move by Doug was totally in character: when forced to make a change, don't mess around. But compared to other albums Doug recorded, 1974's *Groovers Paradise* came off to more than a few listeners as smarmy and slight; one of the ablest critics of the cosmic cowboys was now trying too hard to be one of them. The title song wasn't rock and roll, it wasn't country, and it wasn't jazz—it was coy and it poked along. Instrumentally it was interesting enough, but in the vocals Doug exaggerated his drawl and love of the eternal delights of cold beer, enchiladas, cosmic cowgirls, and an Armadillo World Headquarters character known as the Guacamole Queen. The album got better, but in his autobiographical approach to songwriting Doug ploughed up grounds for criticism that probably stung. One of the most melodic songs, "Beautiful Texas Sunshine," began with a celebration of the state flower and its most overworked cliché, a hillside of bluebonnets; then the man in the song got to the point in the second verse. After asking his honey to feed the dogs and bring him another beer, he told her to sit down, he had some news. Despite the beauty of the day and the fact that her body had never looked so fine, the time had come for him to leave her. Don't cry now.

The album's ten new songs included "Houston Chicks," "Just Groove Me," and "Girls Today (Don't Like to Sleep Alone)." *Groovers Paradise* was a mediocre effort by Doug's standards, but it did close out with some choice country songwriting and singing. Given a pleasant Mexican poolside flavor with a marimba played by John Rae, "Her Dream Man Never Came" described a forlorn should-have-been rodeo queen who was pretty enough to be Jean Harlow or Marilyn Monroe, but she hopped from bed to bed, lover to lover, until her hopes and looks were gone. The closer, "Catch Me in the Morning," contained fine steel guitar play by Gary Potterton, whom the producers brought in from California. The lyrics, which portrayed someone like Doug trying to apologize to a woman, were built on his patented short repeated verses that were comic in a way, but later you walked around humming, stopping to think what that tune was. "*Catch me in the morning when I'm feeling better / The gig was really hard on my head last night.*"

Doug in cutoff jeans with Texas friends. Jack Barber on the far right, Garry P. Nunn third from right. Photo courtesy of Shawn Sahm.

That summer Doug and his band and Freda and the Firedogs played at Willie Nelson's Fourth of July Picnic at an auto speedway between Austin and Houston, and the ghost of Altamont raised its ugly head. Nobody got killed, but Marcia Ball went home afterward and sharply described the cocaine-fueled chaos she had seen backstage to a neighbor who happened to be a UPI reporter. Her words got back to Willie's crowd and were not well received. Wolfman Jack and NBC television crews had gotten into shouting and shoving matches with burly security guards. A fire broke out and consumed several cars, one of which belonged to a hopeful collegiate songwriter named Robert Earl Keen. The story would make rich material in the stage act of Keen, and a photo of his Mustang in flames would one day adorn the cover of one of his albums.

Doug had bet on the cosmic cowboy craze just as it died like a crop of plants overwhelmed by a withering blight. One by one, the progressive country FM stations in Texas changed formats. Disco, of all things, enjoyed a brief vogue in a town that had prematurely billed itself as the nation's live music capital, and then came an explosion of punk rock. A PBS executive flew down from the East Coast during this period in support of Austin City Limits and this energetic young rival of Nashville; the program's producer, Bill Arhos, drove her all over town in search of one country band.

Though the song "Groovers Paradise" heaped flattery on Austin and contributed a catch phrase to the city's avid self-absorption, the album did not perform well for Warner, and certain people at the record company did not care for aspects of the songwriter's drift. Just two years earlier, the Supreme Court had made its ruling in Roe v. Wade, and feminists were trying to get state legislatures to enact an Equal Rights Amendment to the Constitution. After swearing to Bill Bentley that Texas was still a paradise for musicians, Doug was not so optimistic about trends he saw in the recording industry. "It's a different ball game," he said. "Like with Warner Brothers, the Groovers Paradise phase, a lot of people in their organization thought we were too chauvinistic and they wouldn't promote our record. They tried to tell me how I was raised and how I have to live my life, and, man, that I've got to stop and be a wimp just because they don't dig it. I'm sorry. I ain't bending. I'm Texas, Texas manhood, and I'm going to play that way. But it did get me out of my contract. That's why my head is so free today, because I'm not owned by anybody."

Country Boogie

s Doug put another project in the rearview mirror and absorbed and rationalized its failure, Willie Nelson responded with more agility to having Atlantic's rug jerked out from under his feet. He spent twenty thousand dollars to buy a week's time in the studio of a Dallas advertising agency to record another story album, this tale set in the American West of 1901 and called *The Red-Headed Stranger*. Willie made his break by working an all-but-forgotten song into his tale about a preacher turned avenging gunman. Willie's haunting interpretation of a Fred Rose song first recorded by Roy Acuff in 1945 hit number 1 on the *Billboard* country chart in October 1975 and won Willie the Grammy for the year's best male country vocal. Also, with his album *Dreaming My Dreams* and single "Bob Wills Is Still the King," Waylon Jennings was voted the Country Music Association's top male vocalist of the year. It's ironic that the ballyhooed desperados of country music enshrined themselves as stars by reaching back and embracing hallowed saints like Roy Acuff, Fred Rose, and Bob Wills. Paradoxically, most Nashville executives continued to ignore them. The only other musicians identified with Austin that Nashville did not then shun were Asleep at the Wheel, the nouveau western swing band led by Ray Benson, a guitar player and bass singer, originally from Pennsylvania, who looked like a basketball forward in cowboy attire. A lively group who had landed in Austin because they could not find work in California, they recorded a hit in 1974 called "The Letter That Johnny Walker Read."

Doug had high personal and professional regard for Willie and Ray Benson, but after making an unsuccessful run at Nashville with "Be Real," and the brush-off he received there even with Jerry Wexler's endorsement, in his heart of hearts he never much cared what the country music establishment thought of him. But he did pay attention to *Billboard* and other trades and charts: not one of Austin's cosmic cowboy or rock groups showed up on any of the commercial registers of 1975. The big Texas rock band was Houston's trio ZZ Top, with their single "Tush."

Doug was market-driven but never one to panic. His new band, which he called the Texas Tornados, was composed of Augie Meyers on keyboards, Jack Barber on bass, George Rains on drums, and Atwood Allen on rhythm guitar and backup vocals—San Antonio hands who had been involved in several of his artistic, though not necessarily commercial, triumphs. He also brought in a tall, skinny pedal steel and slide guitar and harmonica player, Harry Hess, and an acoustic guitar player he called Uncle Mickey Moody. MCA hired Huey Meaux to produce the album, and they returned to Houston and the old Gold Star Studios—renamed SugarHill by Meaux—where the Quintet had recorded "She's About a Mover," "The Rains Came," and *The Return of Doug Saldaña*.

The black-and-white cover photo had them cropped a bit roughly and superimposed against a barren dirt road near a Fifties Cadillac and with a long ropy tornado bearing down to their rear. The stellar Austin photographer Burton Wilson contributed another color shot of Doug wearing boots, jeans, a mackinaw and long muffler, and a hat and pair of slightly tinted granny glasses; he leaned against the prized relict jukebox of the Soap Creek Saloon that had been dragged outside on a sunny winter day. *Groovers Paradise* had come off sounding halfhearted and disingenuous. But with *Texas Rock for Country Rollers*, released by MCA, Doug nailed the Austin sound and outlook as he had in *Doug Sahm and Band*.

Harry Hess proved an able addition. Along with Moody's acoustic guitar, Hess on the steel and bottleneck left Doug free to assert his own skills on the electric guitar, producing the fluid and emotive sound for which Austin music was fast becoming known. Allen's singing also brought back the "high Johnny and Jack harmony," as Doug called it, that had worked so well on the first Atlantic album. Two country highlights were the covers of Allen's ten-derhearted "I Love the Way You Love (The Way I Love You)" and the 1962 hit Claude King had made of Merle Kilgore's "Wolverton Mountain," a song that Doug loved to sing. The band went off in pre-Beatles directions with a medley of songs, "Sometimes" and "Cryin' Inside," that were recorded by one of Huey Meaux's swamp pop artists and an early hero of Doug, Gene Thomasson. The rest of the album consisted of seven new songs, all written by Doug. He had never written much better or seemed to enjoy singing more. In "I'm Missing You," he toyed with the Buddy Holly effect of blending his singing with a play-ful and popular if nonsensical stammer high in his throat—something he'd never tried before, at least on a record. "Cowboy Peyton Place" began with the tongue-in-cheek but plausible confession that he was hanging around Soap Creek one night when the wife of the steel player in the band onstage remarked that Doug's records turned her on. Never mind the fact that she was married— she and her husband liked to fool around.

In the next cut, he started out with an odd high note that was hard for him to reach, but he got there and then, with little more discernible help than chords of his guitar, Hess's steel, and Allen's harmony on the chorus, he sang lyrics of intense loss. A man was telling a woman in San Antonio to take his picture off the wall, go on and keep the TV, he didn't care about the material things they shared. He told her that her friend cocaine was really the one to blame: "*He has drained life from your face / he has taken my place.*" The song was a short piece that the band could easily play, but given his penchant for laying out strains of autobiography in his songwriting, it implied things about his tortured relationship with his ex-wife that no one close to him much cared to explore.

The album's endnote took a wry view of the cool chest-out swagger that held forth in Austin in the mid-Seventies. The song began with a few bars of electric and slide guitar showmanship, then George Rains banged out a tran-sition, and they settled into a dead-on recollection of Muddy Waters's intro march of "I'm a Man." Doug delivered about as good and respectful a job as a white man could of changing his singing voice and making himself sound black. "You Can't Hide a Redneck (under That Hippy Hair)" was a satire of the faddish pretensions in Austin, though it poked some fun at the songwriter him-self. "*I don't care how many joints you roll / Oh, man, you got a white man's soul.*"

Doug taped his first appearance on Austin City Limits in October 1975, and it aired the following spring. The PBS program was early in its record-setting run on the network and feeling its way. Gary P. Nunn's "London Homesick Blues" had not yet become the theme song. The studio did not yet have the set with the backdrop of the Austin skyline at night; it consisted of a small stage, some bleachers, and a bare floor where people could sit and a handful of them dance, if the spirit moved them. Doug and Augie, who had made their Quintet TV debuts a decade earlier, encountered none of the weird choreography of *Hullabaloo* or the goofball chic of *Playboy after Dark.* Cigarette smoke wafted through the room; crew walked between cameras and the musicians. A char-treuse towel that Doug used to wipe the sweat off his face and head lay beside a paper cup of Budweiser on the station's Steinway & Sons grand piano.

When the program was taped Doug was three weeks shy of his thirty-fourth birthday. He was so thin in those days that the word that came to mind was scrawny. Doug wore his customary boots, tight blue jeans, wide belt with a rodeo-style belt buckle, and a blue plaid cowboy shirt with some embroidery on the back and shoulders—an armadillo and a scorpion that referred of course to Scorpio, his sign of the horoscope (he always put a lot of stock in that). He wore five rings, three on the right hand, two on the left, the largest a turquoise rock on his right index finger. Also he had a tooled silver bracelet on his right wrist, an expensive watch on his left, a choker necklace strung with beads of more turquoise, his distinctive flat-crowned beaver hat with a band of silver Mexican conchos, and a circular pair of granny glasses perched halfway down his nose.

The show began with Doug's voice off-camera: "Come on in here, Augie." It was striking how much taller and larger his old friend was. Augie had on the black round-toed brogans he always wore, one with the built-up sole and heel to accommodate his shorter leg and the limp the childhood disease had caused. He wore jeans and a denim shirt with the sleeves unsnapped and a large embroidery on the back advertising his Western Head Band. For years he'd set the regional mark for hippie beard and hair; the neatly woven rope of it was broad as a child's fist at the nape of his neck and tapered to a point in the small of his back. As they stood together Augie strapped on a guitar. Taking in the crowd, Doug held up a fiddle and a bow like he'd just pulled them out of a tar pit. Then he put the fiddle on his bicep near his pointed chin and sawed the

bow through the first notes of "(Is Anybody Going to) San Antone," a song familiar enough that just the first notes raised a cry from the audience; then he and Augie, who was playing chords of rhythm guitar, were singing about their hometown and how if a man was sleeping in the cold in a roadside park, he just might wake up dead. "Ever'body sing," Doug exhorted the crowd. "Woo hah!"

He kept going in that vein in the next song, stomping and hunkering down to fiddle "Cotton-Eyed Joe." "All right, Austin!" he hollered at the end. "Thank you, brothers and sisters! *Don't think country can't boogie!*" Then he strapped on his guitar, wearing it low on his hip, while Augie took a while to get connected and comfortable behind the Vox. Doug dedicated the next song, "The Rains Came," to a woman friend and said that he wrote it one stormy night in New Braunfels (which on the program's airing raised some eyebrows among Quintet cognoscenti, since Meaux owned songwriting credits to the song first recorded by a swamp pop client, Big Sambo and the Housebreakers).

Some of the most remarkable shots in this TV performance began to come from close-ups of Augie playing the Vox, a really flimsy instrument. Augie was a big man, and he pumped hard on the black and white keys, which set the whole frame of it quivering and jiggling.

On the next song Doug changed pace again. "This is for all the people who love a Texas legend, Mr. T-Bone Walker." He dug into his guitar, playing "Papa Ain't Salty," walking around the stage and executing some startling stretches of his jaws and mouth. Just about anyone can open his or her mouth and form

Augie making rock and roll out of the instrument his dad wanted him to play, sometimes with Doug in his country-inflected bands of the mid-Seventies, also leading his own Western Head Band. Photo courtesy of Shawn Sahm.

the shape of an oblong oval, but Doug had a way of tilting the axis so that it stretched diagonally, and then he made it look like two globes, one sitting on top of the other, only they were rolling slightly, and weren't quite lined up. Starting to sweat now, he nodded at Augie, who played a solo on the Steinway piano; then he turned to the fine (and well-barbered) bass player Jack Barber, who thumped through an even longer one. *"Git it git it git it!"* the bandleader cried. The crowd appeared a bit restive as Doug and his band went right into "Stormy Monday." When he sang the line about how the eagle flies on Friday he turned loose of the guitar and flapped his skinny arms like they were wings. The sweat was running now, dripping off his chin. His glasses slid down his nose; with his middle finger he reached up and nudged them back. For this young, affluent, and very white audience, it had the aspect of a tutorial. Here's your blues, now. They're good for you. "All right," said Doug, pleased with himself and the guys, as they finished. "T-Bone Walker."

"How about *Jerry Jeff* Walker?" someone yelled in the brief clamor.

Doug ignored that one. Seconds later he regained control of the crowd with the arresting and sad first line of "At the Crossroads," probably his finest song: *"Leaving you, girl, heading down the road . . ."* He then took a poll of voices on whether they wanted "Nuevo Laredo" or "Mendocino." It sounded like they closely favored the latter, but if so, it was Doug's show, and he overruled them. With a sweep of his arm he offered, "This one's for all of us little boys who grew up in Texas. Playing football on Friday night. Nineteen sixty-five, start growing your hair a little long, we'd go down there and they'd be yelling, 'Ringo! Hey, Ringo!' They thought we all looked like the Beatles. Well, times change, don't they?" Then they were off in the silly, racing song, once more paced by Augie's Vox and Doug's spirited voice, and without one traditional instrument they somehow made it sound Mexican (it was the Vox mimicking an accordion). For the first time young women gathered up front, clearing room to dance to a song about men getting drunk and flirting with danger in a border town, lyrics graced, as they often were in Doug's writing, by repetitions of one memorable line, *"in the night with all its glory."*

More dancers crowded up front for "Dynamite Woman"; then people started yelling, "West Side," and Doug grinned and accommodated with a medley. To him those words suggested a period of time and state of mind, not just one place on earth. Doug began the medley with "Crazy, Crazy Baby," a swamp pop number by Larry Lange and His Lonely Knights, a Gulf Coast Fifties group who prided themselves on their ducktail haircuts, and the arrangement would find its way back to that song at the end, but in almost seamless fashion he visited Gene Thomasson's "Sometimes" and Freddy Fender's "Wasted Days and Wasted Nights," which drew a roar of approval from the crowd. But the explosion of sheer joy came halfway through the medley when Augie played a piano solo and Doug segued off that into some verses of the Elvis Presley song "One Night." You could see it and hear it on TV without having been there: as Bobby Earl Smith had described him covering a Rolling Stones song one night at the Split Rail, for a few seconds it was as if the excitement caused the walls to take in a large gulp of air. As Augie grinned and banged away on the piano, Doug wagged his bony legs inward and out, turned his head and sang over his shoulder and granny glasses, down his arm; amid whoops out front he grabbed the mike and made love to the inane lyrics with his prehensile mouth. *"Always lived a very quiet life / I ain't never did no wrong."*

Sometimes I Cry

n 1976 the San Antonio radio station KSYM featured Doug and his new band and album on a program sponsored by the U.S. Army Reserve called *Country Cookin'*. The old rockabilly Conway Twitty had contributed a desperately upbeat advertising ditty that went, "*You earn when you serve in the Army Reserve / and part of what you earn is pride.*" The disk jockey, Lee Coleman, gushed with praise for Doug's life story and his new record and country-oriented sound. Doug breezed on about his country roots as a boy growing up in San Antonio, and then he theorized about the growing receptivity to country of an audience where it might be unexpected. He observed that the famous beat poet Allen Ginsberg had come out to one of his recent gigs. That was because of his time in San Francisco in the day, of course. But, Doug went on, if you took fifteen-year-old kids who thought Lynyrd Skynyrd hung the moon, and asked them what they thought of country-western, they'd probably turn up their noses, but at the same time they were learning to listen to it on the albums of his friends the Grateful Dead. All of this may have been true enough, but what a shuck-and-jiver!

Coleman asked Doug what he wanted to see happen for him in the next year. Life was good now, he said. He had a great place in Austin, lots of trees, and time to reflect. His producer Huey Meaux was nearby in Houston, and in Atwood Allen his team had a terrific second songwriter now. "People in the FM field have pushed my records and fed me for a long time, and I want to keep that going," he said. "But I really do have my sights on country, really do want to go on out there with it—do some George Jones tours."

George Jones! *With* George Jones or *like* George Jones? Whatever Doug had in mind that day, he had changed it by early May 1977, when a capacity crowd packed into the Armadillo to witness a reunion concert of the original Sir Douglas Quintet. Augie Meyers was going to record *Live Love* for the Quintet on a new independent label he had founded called Texas Re-Cord, and the Armadillo's very able video crew had been positioning cameras and calculating angles thinking they would be shooting a quintet, meaning five players. But not so fast. With a few words about "the English revolution and all that," one of the Armadillo's front men introduced them—Frank Morin, Johnny Perez, Frank Barber, Augie, and Doug. The bandleader said they'd been hiding out in Mexico for a while, but somebody told them Austin was the place to be. "We're gonna start off with a song that was number 1 for us in England for a while." "Dynamite Woman" was a catchy little song, and as usual they played it rambunctiously and well, but it never charted number 1 in England. That was Doug; he always had to stretch the truth now and then. And if the people who crowded into the old armory thought they were going to relive the San Antonio skating-rink rock of a dozen years earlier they were sadly mistaken.

Just as he'd once made Bill Graham frantic at the Fillmore, Doug sent the Armadillo crews scrambling by showing up with his biggest blowout band— Rocky Morales and the rest of the West Side Horns. He was in the mood for a set of oldie covers. He brought "I'm Glad for Your Sake (But Sorry for Mine)" out of *Honkey Blues* storage, and after an emotional toast to Jerry Wexler, with saxophones and trumpets blowing tight, the band covered Junior Parker's "Driving Wheel," the Temptations' "My Girl," John Fogerty's "Henrietta," and Bobby "Blue" Bland's "Pity the Fool." The highlights were the covers of Eddie Floyd's "Knock on Wood" and, as the finale, Chuck Berry's "Little Queenie," but what in the world was he thinking? They didn't even play "She's About a Mover" and "The Rains Came." It's hard to say exactly when "Keep Austin Weird" became a rallying cry of the city's navel-gazing, but the Quintet's *Live Love* concert album ought to earn a mark on the calendar. "That was Doug," chuckled his friend Bill Bentley. "It was supposed to be this blowout nostalgic reunion of the original Quintet. That's how they sold the show. He brought in the West Side Horns and threw everything up in the air. He changed everything."

Doug's moods were always impulsive and mercurial. Hank Alrich, who managed Armadillo World Headquarters during most years of its existence, told a story about the morning after a concert by the Texas and Chicago bluesman Freddy King, which he had recorded. Huey Meaux, who was back in the business picture with Doug, had some long-standing rights arrangement with King, and Doug showed up the next morning bright and early, fighting mad, wearing his hat, boots, and duster. Even in Austin, the Armadillos thought the cowboy duster was a ridiculous costume in the late 1970s. Doug chewed Alrich out at length for what he considered to be a serious breach of ethics. "Okay, okay!" Alrich finally cried. "Go talk to Huey, and see what he wants to do." Doug came back after lunch wearing a bright Hawaiian shirt, in a cheery mood. "Huey says you got some great stuff."

The Armadillo concert and album and the blowup over the taping of Freddy King may have been just an indicator of Doug's chronic volatility and erratic attention span, but he also possessed a keen instinct for fluctuating audience and markets. By 1977, the Texas cosmic cowboy music vogue had shown signs of catching on nationally. At the apex of the fad, in the movie *Urban Cowboy* John Travolta would be seen dancing the two-step and testing his manhood riding mechanical bulls in a setting of a pipe-town suburb of Houston. In Texas music, Willie Nelson built on the foundation of *The Red-Headed Stranger* and "Blue Eyes Crying in the Rain" with an idea that many country music professionals told him was preposterous. That year he applied his jazzy laconic style to songs by the Gershwin brothers, Hoagy Carmichael, Duke Ellington, and Irving Berlin, and the outcome made him a global phenomenon for the rest of his life. If worldwide adulation was the measure, *Stardust* vaulted him past Blind Lemon Jefferson, Leadbelly, Buddy Holly, Roy Orbison, Janis Joplin, Freddy Fender, Doug Sahm, and any other singer Texas had produced.

That same year, Willie and Waylon Jennings recorded a hit duet on the country charts called "Luckenbach, Texas (Back to the Basics of Love)," which had a line that summed up public perception of Austin music from afar: "Willie and Waylon and the boys." Jerry Jeff Walker and the Lost Gonzo Band were the only recording artists who ever spent much time in Hondo Crouch's Hill Country village, and Jennings never lived anywhere close to Austin. And out on the hill above Soap Creek Saloon, Doug had far too much ego and pride to sit still for being categorized as one of Willie and Waylon's "boys."

In the course of those afternoons when Doug dropped by Soap Creek for a beer, he and Speedy Sparks became good friends. Speedy knew he didn't want to devote too much more of his life to pouring draft beers and mixing gin and tonics. One day Doug told him he could use some help. He and his band were going on the road with the New Riders of the Purple Sage. Speedy jumped at the chance of being a roadie just for the experience. He pretty much got what he wanted from the investment. "To me it was worth it, just to see how it all worked. Getting to watch Big Joe Turner, musicians like that." Also the money wasn't bad, though he added, "Doug could be very difficult on the road. He had to have this; he had to have that. If he didn't have air-conditioning, he'd freak out. Doug would freak out a lot. He would walk in a hotel lobby and tell the clerk, 'Sahm. Single. First floor.' People would just stare at him. What's with this guy?"

The buzz and push Doug had gotten from *Groovers Paradise* and *Texas Rock for Country Rollers* waned after about a year, and his local reputation suddenly took a hard belly punch. Frank Rodarte was one of his old San Antonio pals, one of the West Side Horns. He took pride in being called a jalapeño saxophone player and bragged on the unofficial group as "a bunch of beaners with soul." He was the only San Antonio player Doug had hired for *Groovers Paradise,* and the cover's graphics credited him for "Chicano trips of all kinds." But in 1978 Rodarte wrote a blistering and sarcastic letter to the *Austin Sun* about Doug's mistreatment and underpayment of his side players. The letter made Doug out as a skinflint, at best.

He went back to California to record his next album, *Hell of a Spell,* and his friend Dan Healy, the control room wizard of the Grateful Dead, joined him in the engineering and mixing. The album was dedicated to Doug's hero Eddie Jones—Guitar Slim. Healy said, "In the 'Mendocino' and other days I'd worked with him in San Francisco, there was always this buzz, this push to punch the right buttons and make a hit. This music was closer to his heart. You could

really hear that in the title track and 'Hangin' On by a Thread.'" Reviews were almost reverent. Though it caused little commercial stir in Texas or anywhere else, *Hell of a Spell* was one of his most accomplished albums. Not incorrectly, Doug began to think he was taken for granted in Austin. Out of necessity he went back to playing the clubs and outlying towns. For an amp hauler and sound checker, that was a lot of work for very little money, so he and Speedy Sparks amicably parted ways for a while.

Speedy had gotten a bass guitar and started playing again for the first time since he was in teen garage bands in Houston. One of the things he did to learn was to search out used-record stores and find all the old Mercury LPs of the Quintet, and then he played along with the songs in his apartment.

Then he caught on playing gigs with an energetic youth who was born Joe Teusch in Dumas—a Panhandle town immortalized, somewhat, by the swing-era song "Ding Dong Daddy (from Dumas)" recorded by, among many others, Arthur Godfrey and Bob Wills. The young blond rocker, who had a beaming and cheeky little-boy smile, renamed himself Joe "King" Carrasco, borrowing the surname from Fred Gomez Carrasco, a San Antonio heroin kingpin believed to have murdered dozens of rivals and underlings in his trade in South Texas and northern Mexico. Serving a life term in Texas, he expired in a bloody

Doug, second from left, knocking back with friends at the mansion above Soap Creek. Photo courtesy of Shawn Sahm.

shootout, along with two female librarians he and two other convicts had taken hostage, in an attempted prison break in Huntsville in 1974. If Joe's choice of honorifics seemed antisocial and at odds with his amiable personality, well, that was consistent with New Wave, and New Wave was in. People who didn't know what that expression meant and saw the spiked hair and safety pins in the earlobes called it punk rock. All this multidimensional change was fine for the old pro and chameleon Doug Sahm.

Though Joe "King" Carrasco's base was Austin, he delved deeply into the culture of San Antonio. It was not the menace of drug lords that turned him on—it was the Sir Douglas Quintet. His first band was El Molino, and their self-released album, which was later picked up and distributed by Big Beat Records, was called *Tex-Mex Rock & Roll.* They played in a university area punk joint called Raul's; Carrasco's specialty was climbing up on the amps and taking a swan dive into the adoring crowd. He later put together another band, Joe "King" Carrasco and the Crowns, who went as far in the business as a contract with the major label MCA. The journalist Joe Nick Patoski took a leave from his writing career to manage the band for a couple of years, and his wife, Kris Cummings, was the keyboard player until a serious auto accident and a yearning to start their family persuaded her to retire. The look was Diane Keaton's Annie Hall in lavender socks and pumps, and the sound was the closest anyone ever came to approximating Augie Meyers. They weren't the only New Wave musicians tipping their hats to the Sir Douglas Quintet. Across the Atlantic another compelling tribute came from an organ-driven English-Irish rocker, Elvis Costello (not his real name either), and his band the Attractions.

Speedy didn't stay with Carrasco to the heights of his run. Instead, he improved enough that he found himself working for several years into the rotation of Doug's bass players. "Doug wasn't changing what he played very much, but he was doing it with fewer and fewer players. When I came along, a lot of players in Austin were getting kind of snobbish. Blues players frowned on the country players. Country players frowned on the blues players. Jazz players frowned on everybody. Suddenly rock and roll was kind of put out to pasture. He had some kind of a deal he needed to get done—Doug Does Christmas, maybe a Quintet record. Why, hell, I knew how to play that stuff. And I loved it. To me, playing 'She's About a Mover' and 'Dynamite Woman' was about as cool as it got. I'd get chill bumps."

I asked him what drove Doug as a musician.

"He never stopped looking for some kind of hit single. Never did. Because when you get raised in the Huey P. Meaux school, every record is a project that's supposed to make a hit. It's not part of a repertoire that you're building so you can perform your gigs at night. When I was going to college in East Texas, the original Quintet played a show in Shreveport with the Byrds, and I went over to see them. They played 'She's About a Mover,' and then went into this set that basically covered the songs of the Animals. I mean, the Animals were fine, but why didn't Doug have the band playing their own songs? It's not like the songs he wrote weren't good. When I got to know him, I asked him about that one time, and he gave me a look that was just baffled.

"He loved to sing an old Gene Thomasson song from the Huey P. days that went 'Sometimes I cry when I'm lonely / sometimes I cry when I'm blue . . .' He'd go on and on about 'Sometimes.' I got where I could play that song in my sleep. So one night Gene Thomasson came out to one of our gigs at the Hole in the Wall. I asked Gene if he could come up with us and play that song, and he said, no, he just recorded it. That's how it was in those days. If a project flopped, there was no reason to go back there. If a song wasn't a number 1 hit, it was like it didn't exist. I had to hit Doug over the head to get him to play 'Nuevo Laredo.'

"Our gigs could be pretty tense and chaotic right up to the minute we got started. But Doug was magic when he got going up there. He and Rocky Morales were the only two guys I played with who really understood what we were supposed to be doing. A lot of musicians, you watch them and you think, yeah, that's all right, that's good, maybe that's better than good. But that's not magic. You know it and they know it. They're just going by the numbers. Doug understood the magic. He knew how to call the magic out of those songs."

Wanderlust

The video began with a scene shot on a rural Pacific coastline—on a sun-washed day a pretty dark-haired woman in designer jeans, sweater, muffler, and boots is hitchhiking with a small suitcase. "Teeny-bopper, my teenage lover," the opening lines of "Mendocino," come up and then fade as the driver of a blue Corvair convertible carrying five men pulls over to pick her up. She's no teenager, and she has an expensive haircut. The video supports a Sir Douglas Quintet single, "Down on the Border," released in 1981, but the car is, yes, a Corvair, the unloved General Motors experiment that inspired Ralph Nader's book *Unsafe at Any Speed* and launched his career as an American consumer advocate and scold. Augie drives the squat little car, which has California tags. Doug is a handsome forty-year-old now—a little old to be reviving past hits about teenagers. He's exchanged his cowboy hat for a short-billed sea-faring cap, and he scoots over in the front seat to make room for the hitchhiker. The other three members of the latest Quintet are squeezed in the back seat.

Augie reaches over and dials the Chevy AM dial and brings up "Down on the Border." It's not much of a single to hang an album release on, but within a couple of verses the hitchhiker's long-fingered pretty hand is giving Doug's

Loss of Groovers Paradise. Doug did not always like what he saw of Austin after the Soap Creek period. He took his business and music abroad to Scandinavia and Canada. Photo courtesy of Shawn Sahm.

thigh a slow sexy rub. In flashback we learn that she's on the run from some murderous overweight coke dealers in leisure suits who chase her through a subway station, armed with pistols and grenades. This being fiction, no cops with body armor and submachine guns come running when they hurl a grenade and set off an explosion in the tunnel. Back again with the band, Doug's cowboy hat reappears, and the Quintet play a bit more of the song on some bandstand. Later, the fugitive is drinking beer and sitting with Doug in some bar. Tanked up and feeling loose, she shakes her bountiful hair and sings along with Doug: "*I'm a New York boy born and raised / Wanta go down South where I can get crazed.*"

The South being referenced is Mexico, and there's a brief travelogue of images that indicate someplace like Puerto Vallarta. Otherwise the song doesn't convey much yearning and admiration for Mexico, but the musicians accept the mission of delivering her to safety down there. The bad guys pick up the trail, of course, and the video becomes a chase scene. Augie is grinning and yanking the wheel like some crazed contestant in a destruction derby, with their pursuers in an old Lincoln close behind.

It's the kind of driving that regularly sent the rear-engine Corvairs spinning and rolling. They couldn't top more than about 70 miles an hour, which gives the video's conceit a weird kind of charm. The Lincoln overtakes the chugging little convertible, and the hitchhiker pops open her suitcase and hurls a grenade of her own. When the Lincoln blows through the smoke and flash of that explosion she starts throwing cellophane-wrapped bags of white powder that we understand is cocaine. She's being chased because she had earlier swiped their loot. The bad guys screech to a halt when they see their ill-gotten fortune splashed like flour on the hood of their car. Then as "Down on the Border" wanes there's a crack of thunder, and they wail and pound their fists and foreheads on the hood in anguish as the rainstorm washes the coke all away.

It was a new day in pop music, the zenith of MTV, and singles needed videos to get on the radio and have a chance at becoming hit songs. The video was financed by the Quintet's American and Swiss labels, Takoma and Sonet. As acknowledged by the title of a new Quintet album *Border Wave,* the fondness that New Wave artists like Elvis Costello had expressed for the music of the Sir Douglas Quintet represented an opportunity for a market rebound that Doug's records had lacked for a decade. All the members of the original Quintet weren't available for the comeback. *Border Wave* contained none of the

old Quintet songs, it made no attempt to employ synthesizers and other giz-
mos of New Wave rock, and it only hinted at the Tex-Mex heritage that Doug,
Augie, and Johnny Perez knew so well. They got an obvious kick out of covering
the Kinks' "Who'll Be the Next in Line" and Roky Erickson's "You're Gonna
Miss Me," and Doug introduced one song, "I Keep Wishing for You," that remained and belonged in his unofficial repertoire. If fans in Texas had begun to
wonder what ever happened to Doug Sahm, it was because they weren't tuned
in to his big splash in New York.

Jann Wenner had moved the offices of *Rolling Stone* to New York in 1977,
but the magazine still had a great deal of enthusiasm for Doug Sahm. With the
tag line "Cashing in on 'Nuevo Wavo,'" the magazine announced that the Sir
Douglas Quintet was back—yet again. The band recorded in Greenwich Village
at the famed Electric Lady Studios, built by Jimi Hendrix. They performed in
Central Park with the Pretenders and, during the last week of recording, had
Johnny Winter in the studio playing guitar with them. During one celebratory

Doug wearing his famous duster and playing in Austin with Shawn,
at left, on guitar. Photo by J. Carrico, courtesy of Shawn Sahm.

moment Winter threw his arm around Shawn Sahm, now a regular member of his dad's band, and said it was wonderful that they were being allowed to make this great music with just "the old guys." Shawn was then sixteen, dazzled by it all.

The most interesting aspect of Doug's music in the early Eighties was what he did with the band's personnel. Except for that one time with Bob Dylan at the Atlantic sessions in New York, Doug had never been eager to share the limelight with another singer. But now he started bringing in friends who could sing as well as or better than he could. First came Alvin Crow, who grew up with some classical violin training in Oklahoma City and initially made his mark in country music in the Texas Panhandle town of Amarillo. He had arrived in Austin in the mid-Seventies. He wore a cowboy hat at his gigs, played the fiddle with rambunctious style, and gathered a popular nouveau western swing band around him called the Pleasant Valley Boys. Because of airplay on the FM stations, many people in Crow's adopted hometown knew him only for his recording of a song about the convenient properties of a downer found in Nyquil cold medicine. But his music was more complicated and ambitious than that, and he and Doug became great friends. Doug would join him at gigs at a low-ceilinged country dance hall called the Broken Spoke, where they performed country fiddle duets, and now and then, Doug would play the steel guitar—about the only times he played the steel in public since he had ceased being Little Doug Sahm. Alvin Crow was one of the best players on Doug's softball team, the Soap Creek Bombers. He was a muscular guy, and he liked to show off his physique wearing shirts with the sleeves cut off. When he took off his cowboy hat, played a guitar, and started jumping around onstage with Doug, suddenly the Quintet had someone with an exceptional take on Buddy Holly.

Real estate was booming in Austin in those years. Westlake Hills became exclusive and pricey, forcing Soap Creek Saloon to move out to north Austin to the site of the old Skyline Country Club, and Doug's rented mansion eventually went on the market. After that Doug moved from one apartment or duplex to another. The city was changing in ways that repelled him. He went for drives in Austin now and saw construction cranes and office towers in place of funky little neighborhoods that, in his opinion, had given the town much of its soul. On the subject of Austin, he became a somewhat irascible grump. Doug complained to Augie that one night he and one of their friends had a gig at a bar downtown. They were backstage having a smoke, bothering nobody in their opinion, when the young manager of the bar stormed in the room and told them to put that thing out, he didn't want them stinking up his place with their dope—if they had to use drugs, fine, snort some coke like everybody else. "Man, when Austin changed," Augie told me, "it changed overnight. We used to say it was the yuppies and all the cocaine."

People called Doug the Musical Mayor of Austin, yet more and more he felt undervalued there. The rock critic and historian Ed Ward had landed in the city; he had written about Doug faithfully in *Rolling Stone* in the San Francisco days and contributed liner notes for several of his albums. He was a good sport about being conned into believing and writing that Doug's family was Lebanese. But he aggravated Doug. Ward could be abrupt and sour, and he took digs at Doug for records flawed by sloppiness. Ward now covered the music scene for the *Austin Chronicle,* and they got into a public spat that culminated with Doug printing and handing out bumper stickers that read "Dump Ed Ward." Finally they arranged a meeting and peace conference of sorts in the beer garden of Armadillo World Headquarters. (Doug later acknowledged that his crusade had been a little ungrateful.) Ward moved on to Germany and France and provided sterling work for an audience back in the States as a rock critic for National Public Radio.

Doug never had a manager who was anything more than a glorified roadie. He ran his own business on erratic instinct and his tremendous drive. In the *Honkey Blues* days he had written a song that longed for Europe, "Goodbye, San Francisco, Hello, Amsterdam," and in giving half his *Border Wave* business to the Sonet label, he started booking regular tours on the other side of the Atlantic; over there, he found he was treated like the rock star he had been and still believed himself to be. Though the venues were small, the receptions were ecstatic. In Europe Doug found himself billed as the equal of Stevie Wonder and Bruce Springsteen. "He'd go over for two months or so, and then come back over here," said Augie. "I finally got tired of that and just stayed in Stockholm for eighteen months."

Doug's children never thought of him as an expatriate during those years. And Shawn, now seventeen, was the small kid with long hair who played guitar and sang backup with the band. In October 1982 *Rolling Stone* published a

photo and short piece about Doug playing with the son who had been perched on his lap in that 1968 cover. "I'll be honest," Shawn told the magazine's writer. "I want to be a star. I love the lifestyle. My dad cracks me up, 'cause he always wants me to go to ballgames with him. And I'll go, 'Aw, Dad, I don't wanna go to a ballgame.' But if we're gonna go to a show—boy, I'll drop *anything*."

Shawn was not just grooving onstage, though. He tuned the guitars and hauled around the instruments and sound equipment, pulling double duty as a roadie. On one of the band's road swings they played the Lone Star Café, which was a fine gig. Afterwards, about two in the morning, they were footloose in New York City, still in that zone of having played well and been rewarded for it. Doug, Augie, Johnny Perez, and Alvin Crow got into a cab. It was a short walk to the Mayflower Hotel. In the cab Alvin stuck his guitar case between his legs, but the other instruments were the responsibility of Shawn. He stuck his head inside to get his elders' attention and said, "Hey, why don't we send all this stuff in the cab?" They waved, nodded, and kept talking. Speedy Sparks elected to walk with Shawn. As the pair neared the hotel they saw the others silhou-

Augie Meyers (right) at South by Southwest gig at Threadgill's with (from left) Shawn Sahm, Kerry Awn, and Shandon Sahm. Photo courtesy of Shawn Sahm.

etted under a streetlight, still chattering, but they had nothing in their hands, and there were no cases on the ground. Shawn sped up to his dad and said, "Hey, Pop, so where's the guitars?"

Doug stared at him and replied, "Wow, man, what guitars?"

Lost in the trunk of an unidentified cab in America's taxi capital was about twenty thousand dollars' worth of equipment: Doug's Telecaster that he had used on almost all the California recordings, Augie's treasured Gibson guitar and accordion, and Speedy's bass—a punch-in-the-stomach calamity. They didn't know how they could even continue showing up for their gigs. Everybody but Shawn caught an elevator and went upstairs to get high enough to take some edge off this horror. Thinking his rock-and-roll career was over, Shawn got on a pay phone in the lobby and started calling cab companies in the Yellow Pages. Some people just hung up on him. Quite a few laughed and said, "You dumb shit," then hung up on him. But then in a marvel of human generosity and understanding, one man said, "Hold on, let me check." He came back and said, "Yeah, we got 'em. Cab's on the way over."

In 1982 Sonet released a single that was distributed only in the United Kingdom. "Adios Mexico" was, hands down, the best rock-and-roll song Doug had written and recorded since "Texas Tornado." Still, though the romp had few supporting lyrics, one could infer that its appeal necessarily had some regional context. But Sonet was directing its attention toward Britain and northern Europe, not to making the song a hit in the American Southwest. And if Doug did not give the song the push it needed from him at the time, it may have been because he was making another important change in the band.

Doug and Augie with a young fan. Photo courtesy of Shawn Sahm.

Louie Ortega remembered with a laugh the call from Doug that he had gotten at his home in San Luis Obispo. "He said, 'Louie, Alvin wants to settle back in Austin and get his band back together. I think you ought to come play and sing with us.' I said, 'Yeah? Well, gee, Doug, that sounds great,' and I took a couple of days to see if the dates would line up. I called him and said that would work for me, and he said, 'That's good, because we've already got the tickets for you.' I flew to Dallas–Fort Worth, and they picked me up in a bus hazy with smoke and Pearl beer cans rolling all over the place. And Oklahoma City is, what, two hundred miles from Dallas? That's how long I had to learn the songs!"

The result of those changes in band personnel and the bandleader's peripatetic taste shook out in *The Sir Douglas Quintet "Live" (Live Texas Tornado)*. Both of the redundantly titled album's producers, Denny Bruce and Craig Leon, had major-league bona fides. Bruce, once a drummer for Frank Zappa, had credits as a producer for Ike and Tina Turner, Albert Collins, and Doug's hero T-Bone Walker. Leon had produced albums by the Ramones and Talking Heads. This was the best of Doug's live albums, and it was drawn from two nights at the Whisky in Los Angeles and the Club Foot, the hottest punk rock club in Austin. (Doug was known to say things about punks with spiked green hair that were about as snide as the remarks he made about the Dallas Cowboys, but when it came to the music business, he was a pro, he was adaptable.) In the mix Doug and the producers wisely shuffled the cuts featuring Crow and the ones with Ortega like a deck of cards. Crow's contributions stood out in his fiddle play of a medley of "Mendocino" and "Dynamite Woman," a dead-on solo cover of Holly's "Oh Boy," and vocal duets with Doug on Sam the Sham's "Wooly Bully" and an especially heartfelt take on Bob Dylan's "Just Like Tom Thumb's Blues." Ortega complemented Doug's singing the way Atwood Allen had in the Seventies. He asserted himself in the band's performance at the Club Foot of "She's About a Mover," "The Rains Came," "Texas Tornado," and a cover of a well-traveled song of cuckoldry, "What Were You Thinkin' Of," that Doug and Augie had recorded in 1982. The latter song, along with "Adios Mexico," pointed the way toward Doug's most innovative and commercial contribution to American music in a decade. Doug hit two or three chords on his guitar then told the Austin crowd, "This little song is a thing that's called *conjunto* rock and roll."

They began with a variation of the beat they had dreamed up in 1965, with Doug playing chords and Augie playing the accordion in a way that sounded much like it was the Vox. And just as Flaco Jimenez had shown them it was possible in the Atlantic sessions of *Doug Sahm and Band,* Augie made the accordion a driving rock-and-roll instrument. Wouldn't his dad who urged him to learn to play it all those years earlier have been bewildered and proud?

One could say the rest of the Eighties zoomed past before those seeds of Doug's next big success bore fruit. And yet he was all over the map. In 1982 his Nashville recording of "Be Real" showed up in the soundtrack of the popular movie *An Officer and a Gentleman.* And while audiences in Austin might take him for granted—another one of the roots rockers—the Quintet became phenomenal stars in Scandinavia. In 1983 Sonet released an LP titled *Midnight Sun* in Sweden; the single, "Meet Me in Stockholm," went platinum and was one of Scandinavia's all-time greatest hits. "We were having riots onstage," Doug told one interviewer, with obvious pride. "Swedish chicks running up on stage, knocking me over, ripping my clothes." On a Dutch label called Universe, the next year saw a strange Doug Sahm and Quintet release titled *Live Featuring Bob Dylan.* The title was brazen untruth in advertising, for Dylan was nowhere on it. Doug didn't talk about how that came about; nor did he disown it. Also in 1984, Sonet released a Quintet album called *Rio Medina,* and the Scandinavians made hits of "Train to Trondheim," "Viking Girl," and "Nowhere Like Norway" on *Luv Ya Europa* in 1985. Then came a recurrence, in 1987, of Doug doing whatever he could to help keep Austin weird.

He was back in town for a while and got together with the bass player and onetime bartender and roadie Speedy Sparks, the guitarist John Reed, who had played with Freda and the Firedogs, and the drummer Ernie Durawa, one of Doug's chums from the San Antonio barrios. "We were jamming one night with Willie Nelson's band," Speedy recalled. "When they were just playing on their own they called themselves Too Hot for Snakes. We all got going on a Chuck Berry roll, and a new band grew out of that. Doug got Alvin Crow in on it because he could do all the Buddy Holly stuff."

They called the band the Texas Mavericks, and their record was a celebration of the garage bands they all came from. One of Doug's longtime enthusiasms was Mexican (or Chicano) wrestling. The album cover posed five guys

lined up with their backs to a bar; four wore wrestling masks and another had oversized shades and a cowboy hat. The copy on the cover read "Doug Sahm presents The Texas Mavericks, featuring Samm Dogg & Rockin Leon: Who Are These Masked Men?" Doug was "Samm Dogg," Crow was "Rockin Leon," Reed was "Johnny X," Sparks was "Miller V. Washington," and Durawa was "Frosty." Doug and Speedy produced the album, which was recorded "somewhere in Texas" and engineered by "Dangerous Dennis Dastardly."

With much energy but not exceptional care Doug covered "I Fought the Law" by the Bobby Fuller Four, "One More Time" by his Tribe Records hero Roy Head, and "Mother in Law Blues" by one of his rhythm-and-blues models, Junior Parker. Crow stepped up in "Rock and Roll Ruby," a Johnny Cash song that Jerry Lee Lewis also recorded in his Memphis rockabilly days, and Van Morrison's rock classic of the Sixties, "Brown-Eyed Girl." Crow also contributed a new song called "Redneck Rock." Reed tore off into a lead with echoes of Chuck Berry, and Crow sheared the term I'd coined of the controversy and unpleasantness it had stirred when my book first came out; he grasped that it was

The Texas Mavericks. From left: Speedy Sparks, Doug, John Reed, Alvin Crow, and Barry "Frosty" Smith. Photo courtesy of Shawn Sahm.

about nothing more than the pleasures of young people putting on boots and jeans and heading out for a night of dancing to distinctive Texas music.

But despite the all-out fun and carefree attitude, the mysterious masked men might just as well have named their group and album Jude the Obscure. The Texas Mavericks couldn't have thought the album would generate much commerce, and it lived up to their expectations. Few of their fans in Texas ever laid eyes on it. The record company, New Rose, was a small independent based in France.

Doug in a resurgent Texas period, allied with Clifford Antone and Antone's records. Photo courtesy of Shawn Sahm.

Borderlands

The *Texas Mavericks album contained* a somber and contemplative song called "Sister Terry." Doug had not been raised as a churchgoer or comported himself as an adult in ways that many devout Christians would endorse, but his inner life contained a beam of faith. He struck up a close friendship with a San Antonio woman who directed a mission for the poor and went with him on one of his road jaunts to the Rockies. In the song he asked Sister Terry to pray for him, and reflected on lessons learned from the living and the dead. Halfway through, he stopped singing and applied his trademark style of talking blues to the impression she had made on him when she came into his life: "Back a few years ago, back in San Antonio, I saw this woman in her early seventies. A look on her face—I knew she was like no other. She was full of the spirit—something you just don't see today." The song provided a telling glimpse inside the man.

Shandon Sahm, then in his late teens, was the drummer in an Austin hard rock band called Pariah that had been signed with considerable fanfare by producers affiliated with the success of Guns N' Roses. A band member's suicide quashed that group's dreams. Shandon joined a band called the Meat Puppets, and eventually moved out front on solo records and sang in a punk-rock androgynous style that then had more echoes of John Lennon than Doug Sahm.

Shandon told me, "Dad used to say, 'Ah, you kids, you try to live like we did back in the Sixties. But you can't. It's a different time now. You've got to deal with AIDS and all that stuff.'"

Shandon's older brother Shawn, who had put in time with heavy metal bands around San Antonio, realized what he wanted from being a musician when he started playing, writing, and singing with his dad. Shawn played guitar so much like his dad that it was eerie, according to the man he often called Uncle Augie. Shawn and his dad were pals, soul mates, but Doug mystified him, too. One time they were driving in San Antonio when Doug broke into sobs. Shawn did not recall ever seeing his father weep before. He gaped at Doug and said, "Pop, what is it?" They were passing an apartment where Doug and Violet had once lived, and the memories had overwhelmed him. Doug had some serious love affairs after the divorce but did not marry again, and Shawn fell into the dismissive habit of saying he'd had a thousand stepmoms. "One time I asked him, 'Pop, how can you do that? How can you just leave them?' He said, 'No, no, son. You've got it all wrong. You don't understand. I loved every one of them. I loved them all.'"

In 1987 Doug was only forty-six, but the man who boasted that he wanted to be known as Austin's rocker was being thoroughly eclipsed in that realm by Stevie Ray Vaughan, then a thirty-three-year-old who had won Grammies for his first two albums—in the category of Best Traditional Blues! Not that Doug was jealous or anything, but who took Jerry Wexler to see the guy? When Doug was in town now, he might be found playing to half a house at a university-area beer joint called the Hole in the Wall. He killed time with cronies bitching about the demise of the Armadillo and Soap Creek Saloon. How boring was that? So he'd load up his Cadillac or Lincoln and hit the road. It was time to go see his friends in Oregon or Missouri or do a guest disk jockey turn playing jazz on a station in San Francisco.

One man and institution probably kept Doug from drifting away from the Austin music community for good. Nine years younger than Doug, Clifford Antone had grown up in Port Arthur and come to Austin in the late Sixties as a university student. On arrival he possessed a full-blown love for and knowledge of the blues. He was short, balding, and rumpled, always with his shirttail out. He opened the Antone's blues club in 1975 on East Sixth Street down-

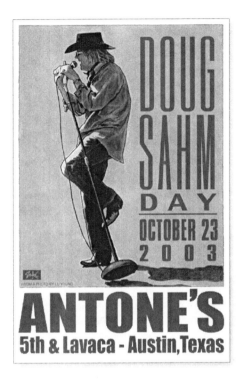

town; at the time half the brick storefronts between Congress Avenue and Interstate 35 were vacant, smelling of urine and rats. The first musician he booked was the zydeco wizard Clifton Chenier. Clifford weathered the ups and downs forced on him by having to change locations and, on two occasions, by getting caught moving sizeable cargoes of marijuana. He was a convicted felon and did some time. But Clifford's sister Susan and others in the club's management kept it going during those periods when he screwed up and paid for it with months out of his life in prison. They were always booking an Irma Thomas or a Buddy Guy and packing in the crowds. Antone's became home turf for Stevie Ray and Jimmie Vaughan, the Fabulous Thunderbirds, and other blues-oriented musicians who set the tone for Austin music during much of the Eighties. Naturally Doug and Clifford became pals. They'd get together and cackle, trading yarns in suddenly different accents about swamp pop and the bayou blues and rock and roll they called coonass.

In 1987 Clifford founded Antone's Records and Tapes, a label with modest aims and distribution obstacles that would have to be overcome. One of the first projects gave Doug as much pleasure as he'd ever gotten from making a record. *Juke Box Music* contained fifteen covers of songs that predated the Beatles and Stones and Hendrix. Produced by the drummer George Rains, the session band also included bass player Jack Barber, who had been playing off and on with Doug for two decades. It was a sentimental journey through doo-wop—that transitional period when youths danced the Forties jitterbug but called it something else and longed for the slow dance and sexy partner that let

Poster for Doug Sahm Day at Antone's, 2003.

HOWDY MY BOY
UP HERE IN VANCOUVER.
SAW CHARLIE AND ARC
ANGELS. IS IT HOT DOWN
THERE? ABOUT 80 HERE,
IT'S A HOT DAY. GROOVEN. WILL
BE IN TOUCH, TILL LATER
ON, BE A GOOD BOY.
LOVE
DAD

SHANDON SAHM
104 ACADEMY
APT. 319
AUSTIN, TEXAS
78704

879 - Vincent VAN GOGH (1853-1890)
Autoportrait à la pipe, (1889).
Self portrait with pipe
Selbstbildnis mit Pfeife
Chicago collection M. et Mrs Leigh B.
Block

© Galerie BRAUN s.a., 1954
Printed in France

Doug's postcard from California to
Shandon, noting the summer heat.
Courtesy of Shandon Sahm.

Shawn (right) and Shandon Sahm, emerging
rock and roll players and singers. Note Burton
Wilson's Pearl Beer shot of Doug. Photo courtesy of Shawn Sahm.

them get in some exquisite pelvic snuggling. Angela Strehli, a fine Austin blues and soul singer and frequent headliner at Antone's, sang stirring backup vocals along with San Antonio's Randy Garibay, and the arrangements were a fitting showcase for the West Side Horns, especially Rocky Morales. Jerry Wexler, then seventy-one years old, sent along liner notes that reminisced about a trip with Doug down the Interstate from Austin to San Antonio: "just another instance of Doug the Mentor teaching his *pendecho* record producer a basic course in Texas-Hispanic music, philosophy, and the exquisite courtesy that is the hallmark of good manners and breeding down there. . . . Some call it *duende*, which literally translates as 'ghost' or 'spirit,' but in this context connotes the very special style of laid back, elegant, self-assured self-respect that Doug Sahm has lived by all his life."

Doug had won the love and admiration of one of the giants of American music. But the Texas-Hispanic music that Wexler wrote about so emotionally was actually quite scarce on this record. Doug would get around to that, in his own way, at his own speed. The only label that seemed to stick on Doug's music for long was roots rock. But with *Juke Box Music* he was making a point that his career was all tangled up in the deepest-growing roots of rock and roll—he didn't have to close his eyes and pretend. And the ambitious kid who once couldn't sing a lick had a voice now that called up with great simplicity and nuance songs as varied, difficult, and cherished by their original audience as Don and Juan's "What's Your Name?" and Lloyd Price's "The Chicken and the Bop."

The critical response to Doug's new direction was extremely positive. But did he get up a band of West Side Horns and other San Antonio worthies and start lining up dates to take advantage of the relative acclaim? Not a chance. Escaping the Texas heat, he took off to see some friends in Vancouver, a city he much admired. He wound up staying in western Canada for a year and a half.

A man named Holger Peterson promoted an annual music festival in Edmonton, Alberta, and he came to Austin every spring for South by Southwest, an annual music fair that drew bands from all over the world and had greatly raised the city's profile in the music business. Peterson, who had a popular weekly blues show on Canadian public radio, struck up an acquaintance with Doug at one of the Austin fairs, and he asked Doug to come up and perform at one of the festivals in Edmonton. With *Juke Box Music* released in the States and pending in Britain, Doug played the Canadian festival on a bill that included the Sixties band Canned Heat and the West Texas worthies Butch Hancock and Jimmie Dale Gilmore. Doug had always fantasized about roaming north beyond the Arctic Circle, so Peterson took him to play in Yellowknife in the Northwest Territories.

An Austin woman friend came up to join Doug some of that time, and he rented a house on an island off the coast of British Columbia. As he usually did during those sojourns, Doug found some first-rate players to jam with, and this time it resulted in a veteran working band. The Formerly Brothers brought Doug together with Amos Garrett, who had played with Maria Muldaur and Paul Butterfield, and Gene Taylor, whose band affiliations included the Blasters and the Fabulous Thunderbirds. They recorded an album in Edmonton with a blizzard raging, the temperature outside forty below. Taylor sang a fine take on Terry Allen's celebration of flat plains and Texas summer, "Amarillo Highway," the Cajun accordion player and singer Queen Ida joined the French howl of "Big Mamou," and Doug contributed a ballad he'd researched and written, "Louis Riel," about a Métis Indian schoolteacher who crossed the Montana border and led a rebellion against the Mounties in western Canada and was hanged in 1885. Doug's song likened him to Davy Crockett.

Doug's standout cuts, though, were back-to-back covers of Hank Williams's "Banks of the Old Pontchartrain" and, with even more emotion, Bob Dylan's "Just Like a Woman." He hung on the pauses and drew out the jabs of poetry in the lines better than Dylan ever could again, for despite thirty-odd years of wear and tear on his vocal cords, Doug's voice had only gotten better, while Dylan's had become a froglike croak.

Virtually unknown by Doug's fans back in Texas, *The Return of the Formerly Brothers* won Canada's equivalent of the Grammy, the Juno, in 1988. Peterson got the chance to take the band on a tour of Japan, where Doug had never played. After a period of saying he would do it and then that he'd have to think about it, and then stipulating that he wanted "his" musicians around him, Doug, Garrett, Taylor, and the band did meet the visa and logistical requirements and toured Japan—and they got a live album out of it.

Doug enjoyed himself in his Canadian sojourn, and he left a deep imprint on the popular music of that country. But he was starting to feel itchy again. He had a new scheme in mind. "Also," Peterson chuckled, "he couldn't find a restaurant in Canada that served him acceptable enchiladas."

In 1988, while Doug was living in Canada, he was inspired by the Traveling Wilburys, a lighthearted super-quintet of rock-and-roll geezers—George Harrison, Tom Petty, Doug's old pal Bob Dylan, the venerable tenor Roy Orbison, and Jeff Lynne, a British songwriter, session guitarist, and record producer. They got the idea for the band and record at a dinner at Dylan's house in Malibu one night and just made room in their lives for it. The band was both a critical and commercial success. The most popular song that came out of the collaboration, "End of the Line," proved to be more of a reflection on mortality than they knew when they composed it. In December that year, soon after the first album came out, Orbison collapsed and died of a massive heart attack in Nashville. In West Texas Orbison had gotten together his first band, the Wink Westerners, when he was thirteen, in 1949. He first hit the charts with a song called "Ooby Dooby." Sam Phillips produced him along with Elvis, Johnny Cash, and Jerry Lee Lewis. The Traveling Wilburys would not have gotten together if not for Orbison's long friendship with George Harrison. On hearing of his pass-

Doug with Boz Scaggs and Rocky Morales at Scaggs' San Francisco club, Presidio Slim's, when Texas Tornados began to take form. Erik Weber photography, copyright © 1988.

ing, many musicians and fans were surprised to learn he was only fifty-two.

Doug was mulling over an idea that projected him in his imagination far beyond the Traveling Wilburys. Ever since the earliest Quintet days the Beatles had been drifting out in front of Doug. He loved their music, especially the early songs that he studied so intently at the urging of Huey P. Meaux, and he envied the way that all four of them forged show business personalities that transcended their music. Louie Ortega told me that the Texas Tornados were born at a 1998 Christmas party at Slim's, Boz Scaggs's club in the Market District of San Francisco. "I was playing with Doug and Augie in the Quintet, and Flaco Jimenez and Freddy Fender were on the bill with their bands. Doug talked them into all coming out together to play the encore, and that jam was like they'd been playing together all their lives. The place just exploded. The guys at Slim's kept coming back and saying, 'Look, please, we have to pull the plug. We've gotta close this down.'"

Augie Meyers maintained that when Doug had first come back from Canada, he played and schemed for a while with Randy Garibay, a much-praised Chicano blues singer whose roots and home are on the South Side of San Antonio, but that didn't work out. "I had a contract with Atlantic," Augie claimed, "and I was getting airplay with a song called '(Hey Baby) Que Paso?' Then one day Doug called me. Said, 'Hey, man, I might have a deal for us with Warner Brothers. We're gonna do it Tex-Mex.' I said, 'Yeah, well, who's the band?' He started off, 'Freddy Fender,' then I said, 'Okay, Flaco Jimenez.'"

In the racing conversational style of his dad, Shawn had a habit of correcting people's memories on the subject of Doug's legacy, and knew he had to watch himself on that, for fear of coming off as a nag. But he contended that Doug conceived the idea full-blown. "Pop was always telling me about this dream he had of forming a Mexican Beatles. John, Paul, George, and Ringo— he had it all planned out. Soon the world was going to be talking about Augie, Flaco, Freddy, and Doug."

"Lo and behold," Augie continued with the tale, "Warner Brothers went for it. At the recording session Freddy brought his whole band. He didn't know what the hell was going on. 'You're gonna have gringos with accordions?'"

They recorded *Texas Tornados* at a studio called the Fire Station in San Marcos, a lively college town between Austin and San Antonio. Produced and later mixed in Nashville by Bill Halverson, the session spread the wealth of

Texas Tornados bumper sticker.
Courtesy of Shawn Sahm.

Warner's promotional photo of Texas Tornados:
from left, Freddy Fender, Flaco Jimenez, Augie
Meyers, and Doug. Photo courtesy of Shawn Sahm.

work around. Behind the four principals, Ortega shared electric guitar parts with a fine bottleneck player, Derek O'Brien; Speedy Sparks, Louis Terrazas, and Jack Barber traded off on bass; as did George Rains, Ernie Durawa, and Mike Buck on drums. Four members of the West Side Horns, led by Rocky Morales, played a song credited to Huey P. Meaux, "Baby! Heaven Sent You." David Grissom, a gifted young veteran who started out in Lubbock with Joe Ely, played acoustic guitar on "Who Were You Thinkin' Of," and Jimmy Day, a star in Willie Nelson's band when they first arrived in Austin, played steel guitar on Augie's "Dinero," which featured the priceless dumb rhyme "*If you've got the dinero / I've got my Camaro.*" Doug, of course, was all over the record, playing electric guitar solos, plunking his one-hand piano, plucking the *bajo sexto* (sharing those duties with the San Antonio veteran Oscar Tellez). The session Tornados were a throwback to *Doug Sahm and Band*—they were an orchestra.

Doug led them through revved-up border rock in "Adios Mexico," then came Augie's rousing celebration of the 1959 swamp pop "Mathilda," and finally the beauty of Freddy's delivery on the love songs "If That's What You're Thinking" and "A Man Can Cry." But the Grammy winner for the Tornados was the one in Spanish, "Soy de San Luis," sung by Freddy and Flaco and written by Flaco's late father, Santiago Jimenez, Sr., an accordion player who was often hailed as the father of *conjunto*.

The dynamics within the band were on telling display at the October 1990 concert that yielded the Tornados' debut on *Austin City Limits*. For all the showmanship and skill of Doug and Augie, it was hard to take one's eyes off Flaco and Freddy, for they wore their sculpted age so well. Wearing a long traditional vest, Flaco often seemed amused, a little distant, shrugging into his accordion solos, then creating an effect that was strikingly similar to that of a blues harmonica. Skinny for so much of his life, Doug had spread out some in middle age and grown jowly. He wore shades under his cowboy hat and a blue western-cut sport coat and a concho tie over his jeans and boots. It was startling to see how restrained he was in this role and band. Visually he couldn't compete with Freddy—the gleaming brown skin and salt-and-pepper mix of mustache and pompadour made for a very handsome man—and no one, at least not Doug, could match that voice.

They bantered with each other. Freddy complained about the band's treatment by Warner Brothers. "*Texas Tornados* is an orphan. The record company

won't release a single, but it's sold a lot of copies anyway, thanks to people like you." He grinned slyly and said of Doug, "This is the only gringo I know who can play a *bajo sexto.*"

Later they were starting to play "She Never Spoke Spanish to Me." Freddy said, "Who wrote this? *Bootch?*"

"Mr. Butch Hancock," Doug shot back. "One of the great songwriters, he's here with us tonight. This song is gonna be on MTV. Move over, Mötley Crüe!"

Wearing a brown derby and shades, Speedy Sparks thumped along patiently but edgily during the *conjunto* songs, with an air of someone wanting to get this show on the road. "Okay, hang on, here we go," Doug announced two-thirds of the way through the set. "The good part of the program. A little bit of Tex-Mex rock and roll!"

The Tornados went on to record six albums, one of them entirely in Spanish, between 1990 and 1999. They played at Bill Clinton's presidential inaugural and the Montreaux Jazz Festival and enjoyed a strong commercial run. Their song "A Little Bit Is Better than Nada" was the theme of Kevin Costner's

Doug playing with fellow Texas Tornado and singing star Freddy Fender (far right) at inaugural ball of President Bill Clinton, 1992. The drummer is Doug's longtime friend Ernie Durawas. Photo courtesy of Shawn Sahm.

1996 golf movie *Tin Cup*. But Warner Brothers in Nashville rebelled against the Chicano emphasis and personnel, which led to their being picked up by Warner Brothers in Los Angeles, which functioned as a separate company. And the divisions and tensions hinted at on the *Austin City Limits* stage were real.

Doug's onetime publicist, Bill Bentley, was a music industry heavyweight now. He loved Doug but felt the need now and then to give him some strong guidance. At one point Doug started talking about easing Freddy out of the lineup and replacing him with Joe Hernandez, of Little Joe y la Familia. "I told him, 'No, no, Doug. Little Joe's great, but as long as it's the Tornados, you've got to have Freddy Fender.'"

When I brought up the matter of the two men's ego conflicts, Augie muttered, "Yeah, tell me about it. We'd play a gig and Freddy would say, 'I got the most applause.' Doug would answer, 'Yeah, but the women liked me the most.' Back and forth, back and forth. My job was to be the peacemaker." Fender was now a member of Alcoholics Anonymous, and he and others in the road crew felt that the drinking, dope-smoking, and rowdy antics disrespected their decisions and needs and threatened to tear them down. Doug responded with his usual tact. "He called us all together," Augie recalled, "and he said, 'All right, from now on we've got the Groovers' Bus and the Non-Groovers' Bus.'"

"But you know," Augie chuckled, "those guys loved each other, too."

Epilogue: Guitar Slim

The Tornados never officially broke up, but Doug's interest drifted, as it always had. In a follow-up to the Antone label's *Juke Box Music,* Doug brought back all the West Side Horns he could find, including his mentor Spot Barnett, who had lain low for several decades. Shawn played lead guitar on an album that with his customary modesty Doug named *The Last Real Texas Blues Band.* "I'm a Fool to Care," "Home at Last," and "My Girl Josephine" were the kind of songs Doug cared to be singing, playing, and arranging just now. "This record was nominated for a Grammy and should've won," he boasted at subsequent gigs. "Lost out to John Lee Hooker. Ain't no shame in that."

He weathered some serious blues of his own as the years moved on. In 1996 Houston police picked up Huey P. Meaux and carried him to the SugarHill Studios. Possessing a search warrant, they forced entry to Meaux's "playroom" and seized a gynecological examination table, various sex toys, a little over fourteen grams of cocaine, and an archive of photos and videos that showed him having sex with girls as young as twelve. Two were the daughters of the woman he had lived with for several years. And then when he made bond on the charges, he went fugitive. He was a storied and important figure

in the history of American music, President Jimmy Carter had pardoned him for his 1967 conviction under the Mann Act, and he weathered a bout with throat cancer in 1981, but none of that would lighten his sentence this time. In correspondence with Jerry Wexler and conversations with Augie Meyers, Meaux did not blame himself for his disgrace and incarceration; he claimed he'd been betrayed in a scathing *Texas Monthly* article by Joe Nick Patoski.

Doug was not implicated in the scandal, but he was touchy about the subject. One of the girls who brought the complaint against the Crazy Cajun had once handled all the fan club correspondence of the Sir Douglas Quintet as its seventeen-year-old secretary. The old man did his time in state prisons outside Beeville, in the coastal brush country, and Dayton, in the backwoods where his swamp pop once reigned. He got bladder cancer while he was inside, and Augie, who stayed in touch with him, said that the illness and pain did not win him any privileges.

"When they let him out he went back to Winnie," said Augie, who fought off his own bout with prostate cancer in 1998. "He lives down the street from his brother, who's a preacher. Says he's bringing somebody along who's the next Freddy Fender.

Before the fall. Doug with Huey P. Meaux, "the Crazy Cajun." Photo courtesy of Shawn Sahm.

"Freddy used to talk about how Huey cheated him out of a whole bunch of money," said Augie, trying to put their complex relationships with Meaux in perspective. "He got Freddy Fender out of the gutter, is what he did. And he got the Sir Douglas Quintet out of San Antonio."

Doug's daughter Dawn was the one who never aspired to be a musician. In San Antonio she married, had a son named Earl and a daughter named Shealynn, divorced, and made her way in the restaurant trades. She told me, "I was home base for Dad. He was a terrific grandfather. He took Little Earl, as we called him then, to the wrestling matches and got him all involved in that. We'll never forget the day Dad brought Andre the Giant to our house to see us. I mean, the man was really a giant"—seven-feet-four, five hundred pounds.

Her brother Shawn described the time in Austin that Doug took Little Earl to see the wrestling superstar "Stone Cold" Steve Austin. "There was this picture of all these screaming little kids, waiting for 'Stone Cold' to come down a ramp. And right in the middle of them was Dad, this smiling hippie with sunshades and a ball cap."

"Christmas at my house," said Dawn, "was just like it had been when we were growing up. Dad on acoustic guitar and everybody singing 'Frosty the Snowman,' 'Rudolph the Red-Nosed Reindeer.'" She laughed, remembering. "One time he decided to take Earl to the mall to see Santa Claus. The man in the Santa suit didn't seem to be very enthusiastic about the job. Dad sat him down in Santa's lap but kept on doing the talking. 'Now, Earl, tell him what you want.' I was watching him and thought, oh no, he's about to go off on the guy. And sure enough he gets in Santa's face and says, 'Man, what is *wrong* with you? You got a hangover or something?' He snatched up Earl and went off to find a better Santa in the mall, and sure enough he did, and we had a great time."

After a gig one night in Dallas Doug spotted a pretty brunette named Debora Hanson and talked her out of a phone number. She was unlike most of the women he would take home after gigs at the Avalon Ballroom and Soap Creek Saloon. Living in Arkansas, Debora was a single mother of two. She was really more attuned to country music than to the blues band Doug brought to the Sons of Hermann Hall that night. She said that when he called and they began to talk and then to see each other, she told him that the life of musicians and roaring clubs was not one that she had ever inhabited, or aspired to. But soon they found themselves involved in a love affair.

In 1994 Doug recorded a new album, *Day Dreaming at Midnight*, that shed some light on his carefully guarded emotional life. The album was on the Elektra label and was produced by Doug's old friend and member of Creedence Clearwater Revival, Doug "Cosmo" Clifford, who played drums on nine of the twelve tracks. Augie, Louie Ortega, and Shawn were mainstays of the session band. Shandon sat in on two of the cuts, and Augie Meyers's son Clay played drums on another. The album started well, with "Too Little Too Late," a song written by Doug and Shawn, but for all its promise, much of the album sounded like he had played a guest session with the wrong band. Still, two of Doug's new songs seemed to address the ongoing dilemma of his inner life. "Romance Is All Screwed Up" longed for the days in Austin that teemed with pretty girls who said, *"I'm the best thing you'll find / I'll love you smooth outta your mind."* The other lyrics described a love affair with a single mother of two. *"Well I took her body home,"* he sang, ever the unapologetic mannish boy. *"I didn't want to be alone."* She wanted him to understand that she wasn't into free love, but she had a feeling they could jive, just like back in '65. The song's title was "She Would If She Could, She Can't So She Won't."

In time Debora and her two children moved from Arkansas and settled in the Hill Country town of Wimberley. She worked for Doug, helping him try to keep his business in order, and she accompanied Doug and his band on a tour of Europe in which fans mobbed them. They went together on several of his fabled driving tours. They drove late into the nights entertained by his collections of jazz and blues CDs and an archive of tapes from the golden age of radio—*The Lone Ranger, Gunsmoke, The Shadow.* (Shawn said cynically that Doug did that with all his special girlfriends—took them to the same Taos, New Mexico, bridge over a gorge of the Rio Grande.)

For decades, since the death of their parents, Doug and his older brother Vic had been distant from each other, if not really estranged. Vic's Dallas company patented and manufactured pallets used in feed and seed stores, among many other products; they were inhabitants of very different worlds. "Debora talked to him a lot about the importance of family," Vic told me, "and I think it was because of her that Doug and I got together again." He chuckled. "I have

above: Doug with Debora Hanson. Photo courtesy of Debora Hanson.
below: Doug chilling out at home, the 1990s. Photo courtesy of Shawn Sahm.

a place in Kerrville, and he got me to meet him one day and go with him to see this guy, one of his old buddies, who was going to repair his windshield. Why did he have to drive from Austin to San Antonio to get a cracked windshield fixed? You've got me. We talked through a lot of things that day, and we both enjoyed it. But I never did know his phone number. What kind of way of life is that?" If Vic ever needed him, he was supposed to call Roy Bechtol, a golf course designer who played and starred on Doug's softball teams.

One of Debora's sons played high school baseball. Parents and other team supporters would glance at the guy with the ball cap and sunshades and do double takes—was that Doug Sahm? If they asked, he might say yes and he might say no. He was just out to get some sunshine and watch the youth play ball. He thrived on his legend, but elements of it wore on him, too. Debora told me, "He'd been divorced and single for nearly thirty years, but he'd never learned to cook more than a can of soup. And when he wanted his dinner, he wanted it on time. Making sure some restaurant was ready to receive us and that we didn't lose Rocky was the hardest thing about that tour in Europe. That, and the time fans were literally trying to yank Doug out of a limo. When we were home, most nights after he played we just went to one of our houses and I cooked us a quiet dinner."

———

Illness was no stranger in the lives of people who had been close to Doug. Augie withstood his bout with prostate cancer, but Rocky Morales would succumb to lung cancer, as would Freddy Fender, who had previously survived kidney and liver transplants. The songwriter and singer Atwood Allen, who at the Atlantic sessions in New York may have enjoyed a studio romance with Bette Midler, would wind up in a bad way, homeless. Violet, Doug's first love and the mother of his children, underwent numerous surgeries for ulcers and other disorders, and she suffered years of decline that doctors never fully diagnosed. Shandon showed me a photo of her in one of her many hospital rooms; she was sitting up in the bed, smoking a cigarette. She passed away in 1998. "She weighed sixty-five pounds when she died," said Shandon. "But at least we knew that was coming."

In November 1999 Doug turned fifty-eight. On tours the band joked about him being the health coach and medic; he was always telling them what to do when someone got sick on the road. But he had amassed a broad knowledge of vitamins and herbs and their use in medicine, and they also knew that one of his dozen suitcases contained the Alka-Seltzer and Pepto-Bismol. Doug was always griping that the airborne mould count in Austin and San Antonio was "off the chart, man." Mould spores, he complained, were the reason that singing to the best of one's ability was impossible in either of his Texas hometowns. He did sing with chronic hoarseness, but that slight raw edge was one reason he sang rhythm and blues better than almost any other white guy.

Doug's older brother, Vic, was the only other person who knew about the childhood heart murmur, and because they were not close for so many years and their parents were gone, Doug could keep that secret to himself. He also had a history of high blood pressure, though he kept that diagnosis from his children. Most annoying to him, Doug feared he had carpal tunnel syndrome. When he started to hit a D chord playing his guitar, the middle finger of his left hand would lock up. In the middle of a song, he'd have to fling the damn finger like he'd been stung by a wasp or grab and jerk it back into working order. He was embarrassed and concerned enough that he went to see a doctor, who told him, "That's what happens to old rock-and-roll guitar players." Cracks like that were among the reasons he disliked and did not trust doctors.

Except for a few last touches, Doug had just finished recording a country-western album, *The Return of Wayne Douglas*—a transposition of his names that, like Doug Saldaña, was one of his alter egos. He brought back some old songs, "Texas Me" and "Cowboy Peyton Place," and introduced new ones titled "I Don't Trust No One" and "I Can't Go Back to Austin." But these lines contained less autobiography than contempt for the state of Nashville country music. The most acidic song, "Oh No, Not Another One," described the parade of country singers in Nashville who pranced out through laser beams and smoke and spooned the public a thin gruel of redneck rock while the people who ran that business knew nothing of Lefty Frizzell and thought Bob Wills's fiddle was a joke.

His opinion of aspects of Austin music was not much kinder. He and Speedy Sparks and other pals would get together and hold an Anti–South by Southwest festival during the spring event when all the hotel rooms were booked and crowds of strangers raced from gig to gig wearing plastic wristbands in search of the latest cool new thing. They called it "South by Red

River." But he enjoyed being acknowledged by younger musicians coming up.
In 1993 the influential alt-country band Uncle Tupelo met him at a Boston
hotel and later, while recording their album *Anodyne* in Austin, invited him to
the studio to sing with them in their cover of "Give Back the Key to My Heart."
He was all cheerful business, they said, until they asked him to sign a form
that would report his payment to the IRS. Doug balked at that; he just wanted
to sing and go. Another time, the Gourds were playing an outdoor festival in
Belgium and had just started "At the Crossroads" when Doug jumped on stage
and sang the chorus with them. The Austin group had never met him before.
That chance encounter led to Doug's contract with the Gourds' friends at
Munich Records and release of his album *Doug Sahm: Get a Life,* on which he
and the Gourds performed the title track and "Goodbye, San Francisco, Hello
Amsterdam."

Bruce Robison was an Austin-based songwriter and singer whose wife,
the accomplished country singer Kelly Willis, was the mother of their small
children. He made a good living writing songs for Nashville publishers, several of them recorded by the Dixie Chicks. He worked into his stage act a lively
country-rock song about a kid from Sam Houston High in San Antonio who
dared to think he could hold his own in Liverpool. Bruce told me, "That record
Doug Sahm and Band is the one I kept coming back to. He was very kind to
me, what little I got to know him. But when I did run into him I kept thinking,
'Yeah, Doug, I *know* you've got all these things going on in Europe. You're one
of the top four or five rock-and-roll singers ever, as far as I'm concerned. I *know*
what an amazing career you've had. I'm already convinced. You don't have to
sell me a ticket.'"

Doug was proud of the way the country album turned out. Both his friends Bill
Bentley and Louie Ortega told me they wouldn't have been surprised if he had
next turned to making a jazz album. He knew jazz very well. Doug was also
enjoying working with Bentley as the head of the artists and repertoire department of a new independent label called Tornado. Doug had been going non-
stop that year, and according to Debora, he suggested that they get away for a
vacation in New Mexico. She told me the plan was for him to go out to Taos,
see some old friends there, and find them a secluded lodge in the Sangre de
Cristos. Then he aimed to keep going and catch up with his old friend in San
Francisco, Dan Healy.

The quickest way to drive out of Texas, heading west, is first to concede that nothing about that desert crossing is going to be quick, and at some point pick up U.S. Interstate 10, which connects New Orleans, Houston, San Antonio, El Paso, Tucson, and Los Angeles. It had been thirty-one years since Shawn Sahm had made a *Rolling Stone* cover at age three, by virtue of sitting in his dad's lap at the photo shoot. Shawn looked like his dad, talked and played and sounded like his dad, and he shot around rooms, skittering in talk from subject to subject, with interior rocketry that was clearly genetic. Shawn lived with his wife Cheryl in Boerne—a handsome old German-settled town that was being consumed by the suburban sprawl of San Antonio. Interstate 10 passed through Boerne; when Doug was heading out west he would always stop by to see them.

Shawn considered his dad his best friend. They would ride around singing and giggling, making up cornball routines and pretending they were the Beatles. But this time his dad seemed unusually serious. Violet had died a year earlier, and Shawn's grief was deepened by the responsibility he had taken on of settling her estate, which involved some sharing of income from the first years of Doug's career. They couldn't talk to each other about those things, so Shawn was the middleman. "Mom and Pop loved each other to death," Shawn said. "They were soul mates who absolutely could not live together." He thought a moment and added, "Also my mom really wasn't into hippies and all this kind of scene, right? Of course he wasn't a hippie when they first got together. More like a beatnik, I guess."

Seated at Shawn's breakfast table that morning, Doug complimented his son on the way he handled the ordeal of losing his mother and settling her estate, then he began to tell Shawn what to do with his business if something happened to him. Shawn was supposed to contact a CPA who had worked with Doug for many years; the accountant, Doug said, would know exactly what to do.

Shawn was startled. It wasn't like his dad to show up in such a somber mood at the start of one of his great escapes. Shawn thought he looked very tired. He blurted, "Hey, Pop, how's your health?"

Doug sat up straighter and bragged about all the vitamins he took. He whapped his fist against his chest and said, "Son, you don't have to worry about me. I'm in great health; you don't have to worry about me. We're just talking, bro', we're just talking."

Moments later Shawn stood outside his house and watched his father gun the Cadillac and zoom off toward his beloved open road. On the way to New Mexico Doug started getting sick. He talked to Shawn by cell phone and said it was freaking him out, that he kept having to pull over and throw up—he hadn't been sick that way in years. A strain of flu had been working its way through Doug's band. Oh no, thought Shawn, Pop's come down with that.

Doug arrived in Taos and checked into the Kachina Lodge. Over the next few days he was sick enough that both Shawn and Debora offered to fly out and drive him home. No, Doug insisted, he was taking it easy, not seeing much of his friends in Taos yet; he was perking up and would be fine. "I was talking to him every day because I knew he wasn't feeling good," said Shawn, "but we were singing songs on the phone, and he said when he got back we needed to get right to work on a new Sir Douglas Quintet record, and we were gonna groove—he had thirty years' worth of plans. That was Pop. He always had ten million things going on."

Doug finally consented that he'd like Debora to fly out and drive with him back to Texas. She was waiting for him to call and tell her when he wanted her to pick him up at the airport in Albuquerque. He assured her that he could make the drive from Taos, but he was feeling bad enough that he asked a hotel clerk if she knew of a doctor nearby. She told him that he'd have to go to an emergency clinic at that hour, and he declined to do that. November 18, 1999, was a Thursday. Shawn said, "I went from a pretty normal conversation with my dad, though obviously he was not feeling too great, to the phone ringing the next day, and a man says, 'Is this Shawn Sahm?' 'Yeah.' It was Officer So-and-so from the Taos, New Mexico, police department telling me he was sorry about the death of my dad."

Discovered by a housekeeper, Doug had died alone in his hotel room of a heart attack. Shawn and his brother and sister were stricken by thoughts that they might have recognized how ill he was and convinced him he couldn't just will himself through this. Debora reeled in mourning and utter disbelief. In Austin, as rumors spread the reaction was one of profound shock. Jody Denberg, a disk jockey at the popular station KGSR, tried to dispel his worry by dialing and listening to the message about the milk cows and Guitar Slim. What made Doug so admiring of Guitar Slim? He would explain that the New

Orleans musician used the same intro for every song, and somehow he made that work. At a loss, Denberg said, "Doug, I hope you're still around."

In his south Austin apartment Shandon Sahm picked up a small battery-operated fan and set the blades whirring. "Made for Doug, don't you think?" he said to me with a smile. He put it down and walked around his living room, remembering. "Dad took me to lunch on his birthday, just a few days before he drove out to Taos, and you know what he ate? A chicken-fried steak. His family had a history of heart disease, and he'd talk about all the herbs and vitamins he took, but his diet all those years was mostly greasy restaurant food. He had all that energy, but it was stress energy. He was a classic type A personality, and one of the last things you ought to do if you're having any kind of heart difficulty is to seek high altitude. I don't know. Dying that young when it probably could have been prevented, it just seems so . . . lame."

Shawn talked of finding himself in the same office of the same San Antonio funeral home and talking to the same undertaker who had made the arrangements for his mother just months earlier. "I'm not talking about dealing with the emotions of losing your father," he described his state of mind at the time. "That's a whole separate issue!" There was a tidal wave of phone calls—opportunists and well-wishers urging them to summon the rest of the Tornados or other musicians to go out on tour and rerecord their dad's songs. But Doug was the bandleader. He always had been. And Doug's children learned that his

Doug and Shawn flying to one of their last European tours. Photo courtesy of Shawn Sahm.

longtime friend and accountant was just as thunderstruck by his passing as everyone else. With dozens of records and publishing agreements to his credit, one of the most productive musicians of his time had died intestate. He had no will.

"Every lawyer except one said, 'Shawn, I loved your dad, I love you all, but I have to tell you that you are screwed. The way the legal system's set up, it's going to take everything.' I was saying, 'No! That can't happen. He paid his taxes. He hasn't done anything wrong.'

"The one lawyer who held out any hope for the situation was a man in San Antonio named Bob Graul, Jr. He'd helped me in settling Mom's estate. When Bob, bless his heart, sat down to try to help us, he said, 'All right, first thing is you've got to find and talk to every one of your dad's girlfriends over the last thirty years. We've got to be absolutely certain there are no other heirs.' I about fell out of my chair. Did he have any idea what he was asking? This man was *notorious*, you know?"

Shawn and Graul would work three years to untangle his dad's affairs with the music business and the Texas system of probate law, but they got it done. Finally, with some studio touch-ups the country-western record did come out as Doug's finale, and it would be followed in time by most of his catalogue. Some of the cuts required vocal overlays. "Can you imagine," Dawn asked me, "what it was like for Shawn, singing harmony with recordings of our dad's voice?"

Freddy Fender and Doug had had some thunderous clashes over the years. But Fender said of his benefactor and friend: "When he offered me a position in the Texas Tornados, I didn't think about it, I just said, 'Okay.' I never had Doug's phone number; that's the way he wanted it. I had to tell him, 'Doug, if you can't stop talking, can you slow down?' I thank God a lot for having known a person like Doug Sahm. He was a personality you wouldn't want to miss. . . . The last of the hippies has departed."

In 1993 Jerry Wexler inscribed a copy of his book *Rhythm and the Blues:* "To Doug, of all the musicians I've worked with, I have always felt closest to you. And of all of them, you are the most gifted, the most versatile, with a musical ability that never quits." I spoke to Wexler a few months before he died in 2008, at the age of ninety-one. "Why wasn't Doug a national star instead of a regional favorite?" he mused. "Who knows? You can't prove the negative. We did everything we could to get Doug and the Quintet in the Rock and Roll Hall of Fame.

And he made it to the round of finalists. But then they opened up the voting to hundreds of people"—he made a sound of frustration and disgust—"and most of them didn't even know who Leadbelly was!" How were these ignorant souls going to fathom the importance of Doug?

Today in Austin the handsome park along the dammed-up Colorado River has been renamed in honor of Lady Bird Johnson, and a bridge has been dedicated to Ann Richards, but the only statue along the shores is one of Stevie Ray Vaughan. Someday there will doubtless be another one honoring the city's international icon, Willie Nelson. The time is likely past when one might have been erected for Doug. Recently, though, a legislative liaison for Austin named Mark Vane helped persuade the city council to name a portion of the riverside park Doug Sahm Hill. His friends and fans like to joke that naturally it's the highest ground along the river.

On a 2006 album called *Knock Yourself Out,* Shandon covered two of his dad's songs, "I'm Not that Kat Anymore" and "Give Back the Key to My Heart." The latter cut began with part of an interview that Doug granted toward the end of his life, and in simple terms he explained the code he tried to live by. "I know I'm fortunate to get to move around the way I do. But I work hard for it. I've been really blessed, made some real successful records, and it's kinda like, the Lord gives it to you—why not take advantage? I mean if you're a good cat. You gotta be a good guy. You can't be some jerk, you know."

Ten years after his passing, Shawn and Bill Bentley were among the producers who brought out a rollicking tribute album to Doug called *Keep Your Soul.* The artists paying homage to Doug's body of work included Los Lobos, Delbert McClinton, Alejandro Escovedo, Terry Allen, Joe Ely, Jimmie Vaughan, and Marcia Ball with Freda and the Firedogs, who reunited for the occasion. The pairings of artists and material demonstrated what an exceptional songwriter Doug had been: Little Willie G. and Ry Cooder doing "She's About a Mover," Joe "King" Carrasco on "Adios Mexico," the Gourds on "Nuevo Laredo," and Shawn and Augie Meyers reprising "Mendocino."

In Helsinki, Finland, one of the city's hottest clubs and roots-rock venues is named the Bar Mendocino. Amsterdam celebrates his birthday every year. Doug's music is not only esteemed in Europe; it's played on the radio much more often than it is in Texas. While the ambitious tribute album was coming together in the States, Augie's son Clay, who had been one of Doug's favorite

drummers, received notice that a Norwegian record company had put together and released an anthology of songs from the Quintet's Scandinavian years. By the time anyone in Texas knew anything about it, the release was a gold record. The man was still making hits.

More than a thousand people came to Doug's funeral service in San Antonio on November 23, 1999. It was a cold, rainy day, with mourners huddled outside the packed funeral home. A lot of musicians came to pay their respects—Joe Ely, Jimmie Vaughan, Lee Roy Parnell, Ray Wylie Hubbard, Jimmy LaFave, and Bruce Robison. "Flaco was heartbroken," said Bobby Earl Smith, the attorney and one of Doug's bass players. "I think that may have been the saddest expression I've ever seen." An array of photographs and a display of Doug's fiddle and childhood steel guitar stood around his open coffin. At the start of the service a radio station trying to feed a tribute from its studio somehow sent through a string of commercials and the first notes of Manfred Mann's "Do Wah Diddy." Maybe Doug would have laughed, maybe he would have cried. He certainly would have known how badly he was missed.

Moving words were spoken by his brother Vic and Doug's spiritual advisor, Sister Terry. After the service, mourners who worked forward in the line noticed that many leaned over the coffin and made a curious, distinctive motion with their hands, as if in a last benediction. They were touching his hat and leaving him for the ride a well-rolled joint.

———

"Doug was like me, maybe the only figure from that old period of time that I connected with. His was a big soul. He had a hit record, "She's About a Mover," and I had a hit record "Like a Rolling Stone" at the same time. So we became buddies back then, and we played the same kind of music. We never really broke apart. We always hooked up at certain intervals in our lives. . . . I'd never met anyone who'd played onstage with Hank Williams before, let alone someone my own age. Doug had a heavy frequency, and it was in his nerves. . . . I miss Doug. He got caught in the grind. He should still be here."

BOB DYLAN

Moment of satisfaction, a rare musician who never had to hold a day job. Photo courtesy of Shawn Sahm.

SELECTED DISCOGRAPHY

Little Doug & the Bandits, "Rollin' Rollin'" and "A Real American Joe," single recording (Tribe, 1955)

Doug Sahm San Antonio Rock: The Harlem Recordings, singles recorded by Doug Sahm while living in San Antonio in the early 1960s (Norton, 2000)

The Prime of the Sir Douglas Quintet, which contains "She's About a Mover," "The Rains Came," and other original Tribe recordings (Demon, 1998 and 2004)

Doug Sahm and the Sir Douglas Quintet: The Complete Mercury Recordings, which contains *Sir Douglas Quintet + 2 = (Honkey Blues), Mendocino, Together after Five, 1 + 1 + 1 = 4, The Return of Doug Saldaña, Rough Edges,* Sahm-produced singles by Roy Head and Junior Parker, and a Spanish-language *Mexican EP* (Limited Edition, Mercury and Hipo-Select, 2006)

Sir Doug's Recording Trip: Doug Sahm & The Sir Douglas Quintet, The Best of the Mercury Years (Polygram and Demon, 1989)

Doug Sahm and Band (Atlantic, 1973, and Warner, 2003)

Texas Tornado: The Sir Douglas Band (Atlantic, 1973 and 2003)

Doug Sahm, *Groovers Paradise* (Warner Brothers, 1974, and Collectors Choice, 2005)

Sir Doug & The Texas Tornados, Texas Rock for Country Rollers (MCA, 1976, and Demon, 1997)

Doug Sahm, *Hell of a Spell* (Takoma, 1980, 1988, 1999)

The Sir Douglas Quintet, *Border Wave* (Takoma, 1981)

The Sir Douglas Quintet "Live" (Live Texas Tornado) (Takoma, 1983 and 1986)

The Sir Douglas Quintet, *Midnight Sun* (Sonet, 1983)

The Sir Douglas Quintet, *Luv Ya Europa* (Sonet, 1985)

The Texas Mavericks: Who Are These Masked Men? (New Rose, 1987)

Sir Douglas Quintet, *Day Dreaming at Midnight* (Elektra, 1994)

Doug Sahm, *S.D.Q. '98* (Watermelon, 1998)

Doug Sahm: He's About a Groover: An Essential Collection from the Texas Tornado (Prime Entertainment/Fuel, 2000)

Doug Sahm: Juke Box Music (Antone's Records and Tapes/Texas Music Group, 2003)

Doug Sahm, Amos Garrett, Gene Taylor, *Return of the Formerly Brothers*, winner of a Juno, Canada's equivalent of a Grammy (Stony Plain, 2004)

The Texas Tornados, with Doug Sahm, Augie Meyers, Flaco Jimenez, and Freddy Fender (Warner, 1990)

Los Texas Tornados, Spanish version (Warner, 1991)

The Texas Tornados, *Zone of Our Own* (Warner, 1991)

The Texas Tornados, *Hangin' On by a Thread* (Warner, 1992)

The Texas Tornados, *4 Aces* (Warner, 1996)

The Texas Tornados, *Live from the Limo* (Warner, 1999)

Doug Sahm and the Last Real Texas Blues Band (Antone's Records and Tapes/ Texas Music Group, 1994)

Tin Cup Soundtrack, movie score that won the Texas Tornados a Grammy nomination (Epic, 1996)

Doug Sahm: Get a Life, with the Gourds (Munich, 1998)

Doug Sahm, *The Return of Wayne Douglas* (Tornado Records, 2000)

Also, these recordings featured the work of Doug Sahm:

Louie and the Lovers, *Rise* (Sony, 1970 and 2003)

Willie Nelson, *Shotgun Willie* (Atlantic, 1973, and Wea, 1990)

The Grateful Dead, *Wake of the Flood* (Grateful Dead Records, 1973)

Rick Danko, *Rick Danko* (Arista, 1977)

Augie Meyers, *Still Growin'* (Sonet, 1982)

Augie Meyers, *My Main Squeeze* (Atlantic, 1986)

More American Graffiti, film score (MCA, 1979)

An Officer and a Gentleman, film score (Island, 1982)

Uncle Tupelo, *Anodyne* (Warner, 1994 and 2003)

The Bottle Rockets, *Songs by Sahm* (Bloodshot, 2001)

The West Side Horns, *San Quílmas* (Dialtone, 2002)

Los Super Seven, Grammy winner for best foreign-language vocal, recorded in Austin (Telarc, 1999)

Los Super Seven, *Heard It on the X* (Telarc, 2005)

Roky Erickson, *I Have Always Been Here Before: The Roky Erickson Anthology.* Sahm coproduced and played on this comeback album. (Shout!/Factory, 2005)

Keep Your Soul, album in tribute to Doug Sahm with Shawn Sahm, Augie Meyers, Ry Cooder, Little Willie G., Los Lobos, Delbert McClinton, Joe Ely, Jimmie Vaughan, Charlie Sexton, Alejandro Escovedo, Joe "King" Carrasco, the Gourds, Marcia Ball in reunion with Freda and the Firedogs, and other artists (Vanguard, 2009)

INDEX

Italic page numbers indicate photographs.

1 + 1 + 1 = 4, 59, 62
13th Floor Elevators, 37, 44, 72–73, 118

Ahros, Bill, 130
Allen, Atwood, 58, 64, 70, 93, 96, 132–133, 140, 176
Allen, Terry, 183
Allman, Duane, 84
Alrich, Hank, 75, 141
American Bandstand, 27, 32, 35, 56
Antone, Clifford, 160–161
Antone, Susan, 161
Antone's, 160–163, *161*
Antone's Records and Tapes (label), 161, 171
Armadillo World Headquarters, 74–75, *74–75*, 79, 100, 101–102, *106*, 114, 128, 140–141, 151
Asleep at the Wheel, 131–132

Atlantic City Pop Festival, 59
Atlantic Records, 63, 83–86, 88–89, 91, 104–106, 108, 127, 166
Atlantic-Rhino label, 103
Austin, Texas, 13, 15–18, 71–81, 87–89, 112–113, 150–151
Austin Chronicle, 84–85, 107–108, 151
Austin City Limits, 130, 134–137, 168–169
Austin Sun, 91, 116
Avalon Ballroom, 43–44, 47, 118

Baety, Leonidas, 64
Ball, Marcia, 88–89, 183
Band, The, 35, 76, 114
Bandera, Texas, 6
Barber, Jack, 28, 32–33, 37, 42, 64, 93, 97, 102–103, 106, 129, 132, 136, 140, 161, 168
Barn, The, 6

Barnet, Jerry, 100
Barnett, Spot, 23, 171
Barton, Lou Ann, 128
Beatles, 27–28
Bechtol, Roy, 176
Benson, Ray, 116, 131–132
Bentley, Bill, 2, 8, 73, 91, 116, 130, 141, 170, 178, 183
Berry, Chuck, 52
Best of the Sir Douglas Quintet, The, 38
Big Beat Records, 144
Big Brother and the Holding Company, 44
Big Sambo and the Housewreckers, 35
Billboard, 23, 118, 127, 131–132
Blieb Alien, 118
Blue Note, 25
Border Wave, 148–149
Bowie, David, 87
Brackenridge High School (San Antonio), 10
Brammer, Billy Lee, 72
Bridges, Willie, 96
Broken Spoke, 150
Bromberg, David, 96, 98–99
Brown, Andrew, 19
Brown, Bob, 72–73
Browne, Jackson, 87
Bruce, Denny, 154

Carrasco, Fred Gomez, 143–144
Carrasco, Joe "King," 143–144, 183
Carter, Jimmy, 45, 172
Chatwell, J. R. "Chat the Cat," 7, 70, 71, 93, 108–110
Circus, 52
Cisco Pike, 67–68
Clapton, Eric, 63, 84
Clifford, Doug "Cosmo," 128, 174
Clinton, Bill, inaugural ball of, 169, 169
Club Ebony, 23

Club Foot, 154
Coleman, Lee, 139
Colter, Jessi, 105
Columbia Records, 62, 87
Colvillo, John, 124, 125
Conqueroo, 37, 72–73
Continental Club, 86, 123
Cooder, Ry, 183
Cook, Stu, 128
Cooke, Sam, 89
Costello, Elvis, 46, 144, 148
Country Cookin', 139–140
Cow Palace, 43
Crawdaddy, 36
Creedence Clearwater Revival, 128
Criteria Studios, 63, 84
Crochet, Cleveland, 28
Crow, Alvin, 150, 152, 154–156
Cummings, Kris, 144
Curtis, Greg, 102

Dallas Cowboys, 123
Danko, Rick, 17, 76, 96, 126
Dave Clark Five, 28, 36
Davis, Link Jr., 128
Day, Jimmy, 168
Day Dreaming at Midnight, 174
Dell-Kings, 12
Denberg, Jody, 180–181
Derek and the Dominos, 63, 84
Donley, Jimmy, 26–27
Douglas, Wayne, 62, 177
Doug Sahm: Get a Life, 177
Doug Sahm: The Genuine Texas Groover, 103
Doug Sahm and Band, 93, 98–102, 107–108, 127, 132, 155, 168, 178
Doug Sahm Big Band, 12
Dowd, Tom, 63, 83–84
Dreaming My Dreams, 131
Dr. John (Mac Rebennack), 96–99

Dugosh, Eddy, and the Ah-Ha Playboys, 19
Durawa, Ernie, 155–156, 168
Dylan, Bob, 35–36, 92, 96–98, 107, 126, 165, 185

Earle, Steve, 17
Eastwood Country Club, 8, 19, 64
El Bebop Kid (The Mexican Elvis). *See* Fender, Freddy
Electric Lady Studios, 149, 150
Elektra label, 174
El Molino, 144
Ely, Joe, 78, 183, 185
English, Paul, 99
Epic label, 62–63, 84
Erickson, Roky, 44, 72–73, 118–119, *119*
Erickson, Sumner, 118
Ertegun, Ahmet and Nesuhi, 83, 85, 127
Escovedo, Alejandro, 183
Ezba, Danny, and the Goldens, 12, 25, 28

Fabulous Thunderbirds, 119, 128, 161
Farfisa organ style, 45–46, 62
Fender, Freddy (Baldemar Huerta), 16, 20–21, 65, 117–118, 166–170, *167, 169*, 173, 176, 182
Ferguson, Keith, 119–120
Fierro, Martin, 42–43, 50, 52, 56, 92, 96
Fillmore Auditorium, 41–43
Fitch, Charlie, 6–7
Fletcher, Freddy, 88
Flippo, Chet, 66, 85, *109*
Formerly Brothers, 164
Fourth of July Picnic (Willie Nelson's), 80, 130
Franklin, Jim, 75, 101
Freda and the Firedogs, 88–89, 106, 130, 183
Friedman, Kinky, 78
Frizzell, Lefty, 7
Fromholz, Steven, 77

Fuller, Bobby, 38
Fusion, 107

Garcia, Jerry, 43, 49, 76, 92, *100*, 101–102
Garibay, Randy, 163, 166
Garrett, Amos, 164
Gary, Russ, 128
Gathering of the Tribes for a Human Be-In, 45
Gilmore, Jimmie Dale, 78, 164
Gleason, Ralph J., 51–52
Goldberg, Barry, 102–103
Gold Star Studios, 31, 132
Gordon, Bill, 66
Gourds, 17, 178, 183
Graham, Bill, 41–43
Grammy award, 16, 131, 160, 168
Grand Ole Opry, 6, 79
Grateful Dead, 1, 17, 43, 101
Graul, Bob Jr., 182
Grayzell, Rudy, and the Kool Kats, 19
Grisman, David, 92
Grissom, David, 168
Groover's Paradise, 128–130, 132, 142

Hall, Michael, 72–73
Halverson, Bill, 166
Hammond, John, 87
Hancock, Butch, 78, 164, 169
Hanson, Debora, 173–174, *175,* 176, 178, 180
Harrison, George, 165
Hattersley, Sweet Mary, *100,* 102
Hawks, 35
Head, Roy, 27, 64, 86
Healy, Dan, 43, 50, 56, 102, 142–143, 178
Hefner, Hugh, 58
Hehnke, Ed, 22
Heider, Wally, 91
Hell of a Spell, 142–143
Helms, Chet, 43

Hernandez, Raoul, 84–85, 107–108
Hess, Harry, 132
Hill on the Moon, 75
Hofner, Adolph, 7
Hole in the Wall, 160
Holly, Buddy, 22, 78
Honkey Blues, 50–53, 59, 140
Hubbard, Ray Wylie, 185
Hudson, Garth, 96
Hullabaloo, 32–33

Jackson, Wayne, 96, 99, 103
Jay, Little Sammy, 19
Jennings, Waylon, 79, 105, 131
Jimenez, Flaco, 16, 93, 98–99, 155, 166–
    170, 167, 185
Jimenez, Santiago, 93, 168
John, Elton, 96–97
Johnson, Jimmy, 19
Jones, Eddie, 142
Joplin, Janis, 26, 37, 44, 71–72, 88
Juke Box Music, 161–164, 171
Juno, 164

Kagan, Harvey, 22–23, 25, 28, 42, 45, 55,
    62
Keen, Robert Earl, 130
Keep Your Soul, 183
King, Freddy, 141
Knights, 12
Knock Yourself Out, 183
Kosek, Kenny, 96, 98
Kristofferson, Kris, 67–68

LaFave, Jimmy, 185
Last Real Texas Blues Band, The, 171
Leon, Craig, 154
Lesh, Phil, 100, 102
Lewis, Grover, 39
Little Doug and the Bandits, 7
Little Willie G., 183

Live Featuring Bob Dylan, 155
Live Love, 140
Lopez, Trini, 32–33
Lord August and the Visions of Life,
    45–46, 47
Los Caporales, 93
Los Lobos, 183
Los Super Seven, 17
Lost Gonzo Band, 76–77, 142
Louie and the Lovers, 62–63, 84
Louisiana Hayride, 6, 19
Lucas, George, 1–2
Luv Ya Europa, 155
Lynn, Barbara, 27
Lynne, Jeff, 165

Majer, Carlyne, 113–114
Majewski, George, 113
Malone, Bill, 72
Mann Act, 45, 172
Mardin, Arif, 93, 102
Mar-Kays, 12, 28
Martin, Mel, 92
Max's Kansas City, 107
MB Corral, 38–39
MCA Records, 132, 144
McClinton, Delbert, 57, 78, 183
McMurtry, Larry, 39
Meat Puppets, 159
Meaux, Huey P., 14, 26–28, 31–36, 38,
    44–45, 47, 55, 59, 64, 86, 117–118,
    132, 140–141, 166, 171–173, 172
Mendocino, 55–59, 57, 66, 84
Mercury Record Company, 7, 49–51, 53,
    58, 66, 84–85
Meyers, Augie, 10–12, 16–17, 25–26,
    28–29, 32–33, 36–39, 42, 45–46, 47,
    54, 55–56, 61, 62, 64, 65, 69, 92–93,
    98–99, 102, 105–106, 128, 132, 134–
    137, 135, 140, 151–152, 152, 153, 155,
    166–170, 167, 170, 174, 183

Meyers, Clay, 42, *152*, 174, 183
Midler, Bette, 96
Midnight Sun, 155
Miller, Steve, 44, 72
Miller Brothers, 39
Monroe, Larry, 92
Montreaux Jazz Festival, 86–87, 169
Moody, Uncle Mickey, 132
Morales, Rocky, 10, 23, 64, 70, 97, 108,
    113, 115–116, 117, 140, 145, 163, *165*,
    168, 176
Morin, Frank, 28, 32–33, 37, 42, 50, 52,
    56, 62, 140
Morris, Violet, 24, 59. *See also* Sahm,
    Violet
Morrison, Van, 156
Mother Earth, 52, 62, 127
MTV, 148
Munich Records, 177
Murphey, Michael Martin, 76
Murray, "Nanny," 47–49, 59, *63*

Nelson, Bobbie, 88
Nelson, Connie, *106*
Nelson, Tracy, 52, 127
Nelson, Willie, 6–7, 13, 15, 17, 75, 78–80,
    85, 99, 101–102, 105–106, *106*, 116,
    117, 127, 130, 131, 141–142
Newman, David "Fathead," 91–92, 97,
    98
New Riders of the Purple Sage, 142
New Rose label, 157
New York Times, 98
Nunn, Gary P., 78, 129, 134

Oat Willie's, 18
O'Brien, Derek, 168
Odyssey Studios, 118
Orbison, Roy, 22, 165–170
Ortega, Louie, 62–63, 102, 154, 166, 168,
    169, 174, 178

Owens, Charlie, 96
Ozuna, Sunny, and the Sunliners, 27

Pammy the K, *80*, 81
Paredes, Frank, 102
Pariah, 159
Parker, Junior, 64
Parnell, Lee Roy, 185
Patoski, Joe Nick, 26, 101, 127, 144, 172
Perez, Johnny, 10, 28, 32–33, 37, 42, 50,
    55, 64, 140, 152
Perskin, Spencer, 73, 75
Peterson, Holger, 163–164
Petty, Tom, 165
Pharaohs, 12
Phases and Stages, 127
Phillips, Johnny, 8
Phillips, Sam, 165
Pitney, Gene, 20
Playboy after Dark, 58
Pleasant Valley Boys, 150
Polygram label, 85
Potterton, Gary, 129
Presidio Slim's, *165*, 166
Presley, Elvis, 39
Price, Alan, 25
Price, Ray, 37
Pride, Charley, 99
Priest, Micael, 75
Pritchard, Charlie, 37, 72
Prunedale, California, 41–42, 47, 58, 112

Queen Ida, 164
Question Mark and the Mysterians, 34, 45
Quicksilver Messenger Service, 43

Rae, John, 129
Rains, George, 48–50, 52, 62, 91, 93, 102,
    106, 108–110, 132–133, 161, 168
Ramsey, Willis Alan, 77–78
Raul's, 144

Ray, Paul, and the Cobras, 114
Redding, Otis, 46
Red-Headed Stranger, The, 131, 141
"redneck rock," 15–16
Reed, John, 78, 88, 155–156
Renner label, 22
Return of Doug Saldaña, The, 64–65, 69, 84, 117, 132
Return of the Formerly Brothers, The, 164
Return of Wayne Douglas, The, 177–178, 182
Rhythm and the Blues (Wexler), 92, 182
Rio Medina, 155
Rise, 62
Ritz, David, 92
Rivers, Travis, 43, 52, 127
Robertson, Robbie, 114
Robin Hood Brian's Recording Studio, 88
Robison, Bruce, 178, 185
Rock of Ages: Rolling Stone's History of Rock and Roll (Ward), 66
Rockwell, John, 98
Rodarte, Frank, 128, 142
Rohan, Brian, 49
Rolling Stone: 15, 39, 42, 44, 51, 62, 64–66, 69, 73, 85, 97–98, 114–115, 149, 151–152; cover of, 13, 51, 65, 79, 179
Rolling Stones, 36, 37
Rose, Fred, 99, 131
Rough Edges, 85
Russell, Leon, 77, *100*, 101–102

Sahm, Alfred, 3
Sahm, Alga, 3
Sahm, Dawn, 24, 49, *49*, 65, 69–70, 80, *109*, 119–121, *120*, 173, 182
Sahm, Doug: and the Atlantic recordings, 91–110; in Austin, 1, 13, 15, 70, 79–81, 112–121, 150–151, 183; and baseball, 1–2, 12, 124, 152; and British invasion, 27–28, 31–33; in California, 13, 39,

41–42; in Canada, 163–165; and contracts, 84–86; and cosmic cowboys, 13, 15, 128–130, 141; death of, 180–183, 185; and drugs, 13, 15, 37–38, 42, 110; estate of, 181–182; ethnicity of, 64, 66, 97–98; in Europe, 151, 155, 174, 176, 183–184; family of, 2–8, 20, 37, 41–42, 47–49, 69–70, 80–81, 108, 119–121, 173, 174–175; and friendship/rivalry with Augie Meyers, 46, 64; health of, 176–177, 179–181; in the "mansion," 112–113, *113*, 119–120, *143*, 150; marriage of, 13–15, 24–25, 52–53, 57–58, 69–70, 80–81, 108, 111–112, 179; and the Mercury recordings, 49–53; and movies, 1–2, 17, 66–68; photos of, iv, xii, 4, 5, 8, 9, 11, 14, 21, 24, 25, 30, 40, 54, 56, 57, 62, 65, 67, 71, 74, 77, 87, 90, 94–95, 100, 106, 109, 113, 115, 119, 122, 125, 129, 143, 146, 149, 152, 153, 156, 158, 165, 167, 169, 172, 175, 181, 184; as producer, 52, 62–64, 118; promoter of others, 86–89, 117–119, 127; return to Texas from California, 65–66, 69–70; on the road, 1–2, 23, 33, 58, 84, 160, 178–180; in San Antonio, 2–12, 19–20, 22–25, 27–28, 69–70, 80, 108–112; in San Francisco, 13, 41–42; and softball, 124–126; stepchildren of, 24, 47–48, 69; studio sessions New York, 91–100, 105–107, 149–150; studio sessions San Francisco, 50, 55, 91–92, 102–103; and trouble with the law, 13, 37–38, 57, 72, 108–112; video of, 147–148; and women, 42, 80–81, 89, 126, 130, 160
Sahm, Shandon, 48–49, 69, *109*, 119–121, *120*, *152*, 159–160, *162*, 174, 176, 181, 183
Sahm, Shawn, 2–3, 13, 37, 48–49, *48*, 58, 65, 69–70, 80–81, 93, 108, *109*, 116,

118–121, 125, *149*, 151–153, *152*, 160, *162*, 166, 171, 173–174, 179–183, *181*
Sahm, Vic (elder), 3, 33, 124
Sahm, Vic (younger), 3, *4*, 5–8, 174–176, 185
Sahm, Violet, 24, *24*, 33, 37, 47–48, 52–53, 62, *63*, 66, 69–70, 80, 108, 111–112, 160, 176, 179, 181
Sahm, Viva, 3, *4*, 33, 66
Saldaña, Doug, 10, 98
Sam Houston High School (San Antonio), 10, 11, 20
Sam the Sham and the Pharoahs, 34, 45
Samudio, Domingo (Sam the Sham), 33–34
San Antonio record labels, small, 22
San Francisco Chronicle, 15, 51
Santana, Carlos, 128
Sarg Record Company, 6–7
Scaggs, Boz, 44, 51, 72, *165*, 166
Selvin, Joel, 15, 42
Shelton, Gilbert, 100–101
Shindig!, 33
Shiva's Headband, 72–73, 75
Shotgun Willie, 105–106, 127
Sir Douglas Quintet: original, 12, *14*, 28–29, 31–39, 42, 58, 85, 140–141, 144–145, 148, 173, 182; in California, 42–45, 47, 55–59; in Texas, sans Doug, 42; in the 1980s, 147–150, 155
Sir Douglas Quintet International Fan Club, 56
Sir Douglas Quintet "Live" (Live Texas Tornado), The, 154–155
Sir Douglas Quintet + 2 = (Honkey Blues), 50–53, 59
Sir Doug's Recording Trip: The Best of the Mercury Years, 66, 97
Sister Terry, 159, 185
Skyline Country Club, 6, 114, 150
Slow Train Coming, 96

Smith, Bobby Earl, 88–89, 106–107, 137, 185
Smith, Judy, 89, 106
Smith, Mike, 28
Soap Creek Bombers, 125–126, 150
Soap Creek Saloon, 81, 87, 111–117, *113*, 119–121, 125–126, 142, 150
Sonet label, 148, 151, 155
South by Red River, 177–178
South by Southwest, 163, 177
Sparks, Speedy, *115*, 114–116, 120, 142–145, 152–153, 155–156, 168–169, 177–178
Split Rail, 88, 137
Stardust, 141
Starmarks, 22
Starr, Ringo, 17
Strehli, Angela, 163
SugarHill Studios, 31, 132, 171–172
Swenson, Doug, 36

Tacoma label, 148
Talbert, Wayne, 50
Taylor, Gene, 164
Taylor, Jesse, 78
Tellez, Oscar, 168
Terrazas, Louis, 168
Texas Mavericks, 155–157, *158*, 159
Texas Monthly, 73, 85, 102, 172
Texas Re-Cord, 140
Texas Rock for Country Rollers, 132, 142
Texas Tornado, 90, 103, 127
Texas Tornados, 16, 132–133, 166–170, *167*, *169*, 182
Texas Tornados (album), 166, 168–169
Tex-Mex Rock & Roll, 144
Tex-Mex Trip, 128
Thomas, B. J., 27
Thomasson, Gene, 133, 137, 145
Threadgill, Kenneth, 72, 88
Tiffany Lounge, 19–20

Together after Five, 59
Tolleson, Mike, 75
Too Hot for Snakes, 155
Tornado label, 178
Traveling Wilburys, 165–166
Travolta, John, 141
Tribe Records, 26, 27, 35, 38, 44–45, 64, 86
Trident Records Studio, 50
Tropicana, 120–121
Twitty, Conway, 139

Uncle Tupelo, 17, 178
Universe label, 155
Urban Cowboy, 141

Van Zandt, Townes, 17
Vaughan, Jimmie, 119, 161
Vaughan, Stevie Ray, *80, 81,* 86–87, 114, 160–161, 183, 185
Vox organ, 12, 25, 28, 29, 34, 45
Vulcan Gas Company, 72–73

Walker, Jerry Jeff, 76–77, 142
Ward, Ed, 62, 66–67, 97, 151
Warner-Elektra-Atlantic label, 85
Warner Brothers Records, 127–130, 166, 168–170
Weiss, Ron, 124

Wenner, Jann, 44, 62, 149
Werblin, Stu, 85, 97
Western Head Band, 93, 128
West Side (San Antonio), 8–9, 51, 66
West Side Horns, 23, *113,* 115–116, 140–142, 163, 168, 171
Wexler, Jerry, 63, 83–89, 91–96, *94–95,* 102–104, 107–108, 127–128, 140, 163, 172, 182–183
Where the Action Is, 33
Whisky a Go Go, 47–48, 154
Whitman, Charles, 113
Wier, Rusty, 44
Wig, 44
Williams, Hank, 6
Wills, Bob, 86, 116
Wilson, Burton, 132
Wilson, Eddie, 75, 114, 123
Wilson, Kim, 119
Winter, Edgar, 26
Winter, Johnny, 26, 44, 72–73, 117, 149–150
Wolfman Jack, 22, 130
Womack, Bobby, 89
Woodstock, 58–59

Young, James "Big Sambo," 35

ZZ Top, 132

INDEX OF SONG TITLES

"96 Tears," 34

"Adios Mexico," 103, 153–154, 168, 183
"After the Fire Is Gone," 127
"Ain't That Loving You," 102
"Amarillo Highway," 164
"At the Crossroads," 57–58, 103, 136, 178

"Baby! Heaven Sent You," 168
"Baby, What's on Your Mind," 23
"Banks of the Old Pontchartrain (On the)," 100, 164
"Beautiful Texas Sunshine," 128
"Before the Next Teardrop Falls," 118
"Beginning of the End, The," 44
"Be Real," 62, 132, 155
"Big Mamou," 164
"Bloody Mary Morning," 127
"Blue Eyes Crying in the Rain," 99, 141
"Blue Horizon," 102
"Bobby's Blues," 103

"Bob Wills Is Still the King," 131
"Brown-Eyed Girl," 156
"Bubbles in My Beer," 106

"Can You Dig My Vibrations," 50
"Catch Me in the Morning," 129
"Chicano," 102
"Chicken and the Bop, The," 163
"Columbus Stockade," 100
"Cosmic Cowboy Souvenir," 76
"Cotton-Eyed Joe," 135
"Cowboy Peyton Place," 133, 177
"Crazy, Crazy Feeling," 23, 136
"Cryin' Inside," 133

"Dinero," 168
"Down on the Border," 147–148
"Driving Wheel," 140
"Dynamite Woman," 58, 85, 136, 140, 144, 154

"End of the Line," 165

"Faded Love," 100
"From a Jack to a King," 92

"Girls Today (Don't Like to Sleep Alone),"
    129
"Give Back the Key to My Heart," 178, 183
"Goodbye, San Francisco, Hello,
    Amsterdam," 151, 178
"Gotta Serve Somebody," 96
"Groover's Paradise," 15, 112
"Gypsy, The," 65

"Hanging On by a Thread," 143
"Henrietta," 140
"Her Dream Man Never Came," 129
"Hey Good Lookin'," 100
"Home at Last," 171
"Houston Chicks," 129

"I Can't Go Back to Austin," 177
"I Don't Trust No One," 177
"I Don't Want to Go Home," 59, 62
"I Fought the Law," 156
"If That's What You're Thinking," 168
"If You Lose Me, You'll Lose a Good
    Thing," 27
"If You Really Want Me to I'll Go," 57
"I Keep Wishing for You," 149
"I'll Be There," 102
"I Love the Way You Love (The Way I Love
    You)," 132
"I'm a Fool to Care," 171
"I'm a Man," 133
"I'm Glad for Your Sake (But Sorry for
    Mine)," 50–51, 140
"I'm Missing You," 133
"I'm Not That Kat Anymore," 183
"In the Jailhouse Now," 34
"In the Pines," 34

"In Time," 34
"(Is Anybody Going to) San Antone," 99,
    135
"It's All Over Now," 89
"It's a Man Down There," 34, 44
"It's Gonna Be Easy," 100
"I Wanna Be Your Mama Again," 62

"Just a Moment," 23
"Just Groove Me," 129
"Just Like a Woman," 164
"Just Like Tom Thumb's Blues," 154

"Knock on Wood," 140

"Lawd, I'm Just a Country Boy in This
    Great Big Freaky City," 57
"Letter That Johnny Walker Read, The,"
    132
"Like a Rolling Stone," 35
"Little Bit Is Better Than Nada, A" 169
"Little Queenie," 140
"Little Red Riding Hood," 34
"London Homesick Blues," 134
"Louis Riel," 164
"Luckenbach, Texas (Back to the Basics of
    Love)," 141

"MacArthur Park," 79
"Man Can Cry, A," 168
"Mathilda," 168
"Me and Bobby McGee," 102
"Me and My Destiny," 65, 127
"Me and Paul," 98–99
"Meet Me in Stockholm," 155
"Mendocino," 12, 55–56, 58, 64, 136, 147,
    154, 183
"Michoacán," 67
"Miller's Cave," 100
"Mother in Law Blues," 156

"Mr. Kool," 26
"My Girl," 140
"My Girl Josephine," 171

"Nowhere Like Norway," 155
"Nuevo Laredo," 59, 64, 84, 136, 145, 183

"Oh Boy," 154
"Oh Lord, Please Let It Rain in Texas," 65
"One More Time," 156
"One Night," 137
"Oh No, Not Another One," 177

"Papa Ain't Salty," 64, 100, 135–136
"Pity the Fool," 140
"Please, Mr. Sandman," 26
"Poison Love," 98

"Quarter to Three, A," 44

"Rains Came, The," 12, 34–35, 132, 135, 140, 154
"Real American Joe, A," 7
"Redneck Rock," 156
"Rock and Roll Ruby," 156
"Rollin' Rollin'," 7
"Romance Is Screwed Up," 174

"Sell a Song," 50
"She Never Spoke Spanish to Me," 169
"She's About a Mover," 12, 28–29, 31, 56, 58, 132, 140, 144, 145, 154
"She Would If She Could, She Can't So She Won't," 174
"Sister Terry," 159
"Someday," 102
"Sometimes," 132, 137
"Sometimes You've Got to Stop Chasing Rainbows," 103

"Son of Bill Baety," 26, 59
"Soy de San Luis," 168
"Stay All Night (Stay a Little Longer)," 106
"Stoned Faces Don't Lie," 65
"Stormy Monday," 136
"Sugar Bee," 28

"T-Bone Walker," 136
"Tennessee Blues," 100, 102
"Texas Me," 65, 84, 177
"Texas Tornado," 102, 153, 154
"Too Little Too Late," 174
"Train to Trondheim," 155
"Two Hearts in Love," 23

"Viking Girl," 155

"Wallflower," 98–99
"Wasted Days and Wasted Nights," 21, 65, 117, 118, 137
"West Side," 136
"Westside Blues Again," 67–68
"What's Your Name?" 163
"When I've Sang My Last Hillbilly Song," 6–7
"Who'll Be the Next in Line," 149
"Who Were You Thinkin' Of," 154, 168
"Why Why Why," 22–23
"Wine Wine Wine," 44
"Wolverton Mountain," 116, 133
"Wooly Bully," 34, 154

"You Can't Hide a Redneck (under That Hippy Hair)," 133
"You Never Get Too Big and You Sure Don't Get Too Heavy, That You Don't Stop and Have to Pay Some Dues Sometime," 50
"You're Gonna Miss Me," 44, 118, 149

CPSIA information can be obtained at www.ICGtesting.com
Printed in the USA
BVOW011218020812

296900BV00001B/36/P